The Emotional Healing Strategy

Gael Lindenfield spent the majority of her childhood in government-run care homes, following which she developed serious depressive illness in her twenties. With the help of therapy she recovered and went on to train as a psychiatric social worker and psychotherapist. This led to a special interest in the prevention of mental illness and the creation of self-help programmes designed to allow people to deal effectively with emotionally challenging situations at home and at work. Gael is now one of the UK's best loved therapists and has written many internationally bestselling self-help books on confidence-building and managing feelings. She now lives and works in London and southern Spain.

Praise for Gael Lindenfield

'So many of my readers' problems – particularly around relationships – are underpinned by past hurt. Now I can recommend *The Emotional Healing Strategy*, knowing that Gael's wonderful seven-step process will help them bring their lives – and their hearts – back into balance'

Susan Quilliam, author and agony aunt

'Gael Lindenfield has written a highly readable book that will, quite literally, help you to be happy. She provides very practical strategies for dealing with adversities that come from her own profound experiences. This book is an emotional treasure trove. I thoroughly recommend it!'

James Reed, Executive Chairman, Reed Executive

'I found the seven-step structure for dealing with emotional hurt a really useful framework. Each step is wonderfully adaptable for hurts large or small, old or recent, personal or work-related. I particularly loved the tone of the book: it was so warm, engaging and sensitive. The sharing of Gael's own story and experience was very powerful and will be of help to others'

Julie Lowe, Organisational Psychologist,
Royal Bank of Scotland Group

'Gael Lindenfield brings us on a journey of healing which she herself has trod. The book is packed with wisdom, good sense and practical examples. It is a self-help book which could be very helpful for victims of crime and abuse'

Dr. Bill Lockhart, OBE, Chartered Forensic Psychologist,
Chief Executive of the Youth Justice Agency, Northern Ireland.

'Doctors are trained in hospital medicine to make sense of patients' stories to come to a diagnosis. But if, for example, a heart specialist meets a patient for whom a cardiological cause cannot be found, it is time-honoured practice to refer back to their GP. This book describes a useful way for GPs to help patients who have had an emotional experience that is affecting their lives. It gives a structure for the path to recovery that the patient and GP can discuss and use. I shall be recommending *The Emotional Healing Strategy* to my patients. Gael's use of her own experiences and strategies for coping will give a lot of readers hope and ideas for their own future recovery' Anne White, General Practitioner

'After a major loss I used the strategy myself with great effect. Now I use it in my work and find it can also be useful for smaller emotional hurts as well. It has been very helpful to use with mothers who are feeling sad about leaving their babies when their maternity leave has finished'
Carolyn Roberts, Health Visitor

'Living and working within a culture which encourages us to get over hurt primarily by ignoring it, *The Emotional Healing Strategy* provides a way of dealing with it without sentimentality or over-indulgent navel-gazing. Gael Lindenfield makes us see hurt for the normal state of affairs that it is. She has experienced hurt, made mistakes, considered revenge . . . just like the rest of us. Her approach is not "holier-than-thou" but neither does the Strategy allow for self-indulgence. She aims to develop our self-awareness and *The Emotional Healing Strategy* provides a practical, usable tool to enable us to function more effectively in work, relationships and life'
Claire Coldwell, career management consultant, career agony aunt and author of *Take Charge!* a practical career guide

'It works! Clear, simple and practical advice that anyone can apply'
Anne Nicholls, agony aunt

The Emotional Healing Strategy

A Recovery Guide for Any Setback,
Disappointment or Loss

GAEL LINDENFIELD

MICHAEL JOSEPH
an imprint of
PENGUIN BOOKS

MICHAEL JOSEPH

Published by the Penguin Group
Penguin Books Ltd, 80 Strand, London WC2R 0RL, England
Penguin Group (USA) Inc., 375 Hudson Street, New York, New York 10014, USA
Penguin Group (Canada), 90 Eglinton Avenue East, Suite 700, Toronto, Ontario, Canada M4P 2Y3
(a division of Pearson Penguin Canada Inc.)
Penguin Ireland, 25 St Stephen's Green, Dublin 2, Ireland
(a division of Penguin Books Ltd)
Penguin Group (Australia), 250 Camberwell Road, Camberwell, Victoria 3124, Australia
(a division of Pearson Australia Group Pty Ltd)
Penguin Books India Pvt Ltd, 11 Community Centre, Panchsheel Park, New Delhi – 110 017, India
Penguin Group (NZ), 67 Apollo Drive, Rosedale, North Shore 0632, New Zealand
(a division of Pearson New Zealand Ltd)
Penguin Books (South Africa) (Pty) Ltd, 24 Sturdee Avenue, Rosebank, Johannesburg 2196, South Africa

Penguin Books Ltd, Registered Offices: 80 Strand, London WC2R 0RL, England

www.penguin.com

First published 2008
1

Copyright © Gael Lindenfield, 2008

The moral right of the author has been asserted

Set in 10.5/14.75 pt Monotype Galliard
Typeset by Rowland Phototypesetting Ltd, Bury St Edmunds, Suffolk
Printed in Great Britain by Clays Ltd, St Ives plc

A CIP catalogue record for this book is available from the British Library

ISBN: 978-0-718-15287-1

www.greenpenguin.co.uk

Penguin Books is committed to a sustainable future
for our business, our readers and our planet.
The book in your hands is made from paper
certified by the Forest Stewardship Council.

To my daughter Susannah, the light that has drawn me through so many of my own dark tunnels

Contents

Acknowledgements xi
Introduction xiii

Before You Begin

 Why Emotional Healing? 3

 Introducing The Strategy 19

The Emotional Healing Strategy

 1. Exploration 39

 2. Expression 60

 3. Comfort 88

 4. Compensation 115

 5. Perspective 133

 6. Channelling 159

 7. Forgiveness 178

Post-Healing

 8. Living with the Enduring Hurt 197

 9. Helping Others to Heal 220

Further Help 246

Acknowledgements

As always, I must start with my husband Stuart, whose constant confidence in me and my abilities has helped every book I have written to become a reality.

For the first time in my writing career I have been supported by an agent. This new partnership experience has been a joy. In the early days of my career Jane Graham Maw was the editor for a number of my books and helped nurture my writing skills. So a substantial part of the credit for any success this new book may have can be attributed to Jane's critical abilities and inspirational support.

I am particularly grateful to the editorial, publicity and design teams at Healthy Penguin who have waited and worked so patiently and professionally through all the setbacks that have hindered this book's progress since its conception as an idea.

I am also indebted to many other people who have given me feedback on this book in its various developmental stages – in my head and finally on to paper over the past fifteen years. Some of these people are family, some are friends and colleagues but the majority have been my clients who have tested out the theory and made sure that it worked over and over again in real-life practice. You know who you are and I hope that you will feel proud that your own healing journeys will now be helping many more people from all over the world to recover from their emotional pain.

Introduction

Time is a great healer.

If you find emotional healing this easy then this isn't the book for you!

But, if your sadness, anger or disappointment don't always magically dissolve with the passing of months and years, keep reading. This book is going to introduce you to a very effective self-help healing programme that will be much more dependable than the miracles of Father Time.

Why am I able to give such an assurance so confidently?

The answer is twofold. First, it was the Emotional Healing Strategy which is at the heart of this programme that helped me recover both my will and my ability to live when I encountered my own worst nightmare. Secondly, it has been the cornerstone of my therapeutic work with clients for the past 15 years. It has helped more people than I could ever recall recover from major traumas as well as the more everyday disheartening disappointments, failures, rejections and heartbreaks.

When my beautiful and highly talented daughter Laura died suddenly in a car accident at the age of 19, I collapsed into an uncontrollable turmoil of feelings. Not only did I feel extreme grief, I felt powerless and victimized. The tragedy seemed such an unfair blow not just to me but to Laura, her sister and my husband. Throughout all our lives we had already been beset with an unusually high number of major hurts and setbacks. Now my worst fear of all had been realized.

Making the pain of grief even more intense, anger and revengeful feelings were also creeping in. Soon after the accident, it became clear that the woman who was at her side when help arrived may have caused the accident. But she had deserted the scene and we were told that it was highly likely that she would never be traced. I began to be haunted by images of that woman seeing my dying or dead daughter and just walking away. The hurt of such heartless behaviour felt devastating. I did not think I could ever recover. I had not only lost a deeply loved child at the brink of her adult life, I had also lost my motivational faith in the essential goodness of human nature.

But I surprised myself. I have regained my emotional equilibrium, my ability to trust and my zest for life. In fact, I seem to have done this very much more quickly and lastingly than most other people I know who have experienced similar degrees of emotional hurt. Many people have confirmed this impression.

During the 11 years since Laura died, I have been continually asked to explain how I was able to bounce back from such a profound emotional hurt. This book has been written partly in response to requests from these people.

Undoubtedly, it is this Emotional Healing Strategy that deserves the credit. It came to my rescue when I was incapable of consciously thinking or remembering what was good and what was bad for me. What was particularly interesting for me was that it kicked in automatically when I was incapable of consciously using it to help myself in the early stages of my grief. The sensation I had was of being inwardly guided along my recovery path. I would experience intuitive 'warnings' when I was jumping too far ahead or was slipping back, and I had a sense of 'knowing' what was right to do now and next. This included who to be with and who not to be with.

With hindsight, I have my theory about why and how this happened. I believe that I had used the strategy so often on my own and others' emotional wounds that it had become an ingrained habitual response. Without realizing it, I had created my own emergency auto-pilot. When my conscious thinking powers failed, it emerged from my subconscious and jumped straight into the driving seat and took control. Although it often felt fairly miraculous to me at the time, there was actually nothing truly extraordinary about what I was doing. I was simply following a perfectly natural step-by-step healing path. And, because I had followed this path so many times to help me through the more everyday emotional knocks in life, it had become a habit.

But I haven't always had this good healing habit. Quite the opposite. For the first half of my adult life I was appallingly bad at recovering from emotional hurt. My childhood had given me plenty of minor hurts and major traumatic experiences, but no help whatsoever in how to deal with them. As a result, my physical and mental health, my work and personal life suffered greatly during my early adult years. After a major crisis and my subsequent recovery, I trained as a psychotherapist and, not surprisingly, developed a special interest in the subject of emotional healing. This strategic self-help approach was developed and refined during many years of experimental work with clients who were struggling to bounce back after all manner of personal hurts in their personal lives and in their lives at work and in their communities.

WHO MIGHT BENEFIT FROM THIS BOOK?

This is a book for anyone who wants to improve their emotional healing skills in order to be able to help themselves or others heal more effectively and quickly. So first, it will help you if you are currently finding it difficult to move on after any specific emotional hurt such as:

- The break-up of a relationship, for example a marriage, partnership or friendship;

- The death of a loved one;

- The loss of a long-standing job or a complete career through enforced redundancy;

- An estrangement from your children due to a divorce;

- A deceit perpetrated by someone you loved and trusted;

- Unexpected failure in an important exam or interview;

- The loss of a lifestyle or life-dream due to unfair or unforeseen major reduction in financial circumstances;

- Loss of trust and sense of security as a result of being the victim of crime, abuse or any other unforeseen traumatic experience;

- The loss of your health or a part of your body.

Secondly, it will be of great benefit for anyone who wants to bounce back quickly from the more everyday emotional knocks in life. After meeting these, we may shed the odd tear, hiss under our breath or even stamp a foot or two, but how often do we consider them worthy of any special healing attention? This may not be a problem for the thicker-skinned amongst us. But for many of us, the unhealed hurt from such experiences can linger on and fester inside us. If this buried sadness or resentment mounts up it can, at best, diminish our *joie de vivre* and general resilience and, at worst, cause serious damage to our physical health and potential for happiness and success. This book will show you how to de-stress your life and recover effectively from these kinds of common emotional knocks:

- A wound to your self-esteem from an insulting put-down, an unfair criticism, a racist remark, a failure, a mistake or a personal rejection;

- A disappointment such as a lost order at work, the enforced cancellation of a dream holiday or a financial setback that has caused so much regret that it is affecting your motivation and giving you a constant anxiety headache;

- The loss of a community resulting from a house or job move or an escape from harassment which has left you feeling lonely and unsupported;

- A rejection from training for a chosen career or sport that has left you so disappointed or resentful that you can't summon up any enthusiasm to try something else;

- The death of a special pet which you miss so much that you find yourself still crying or unable to think about getting another one;

- The loss of treasured goods as the result of a robbery or wilful damage that has left you with obsessive thoughts of revenge;

- A deception by a salesperson that has left a dent in your bank balance and has made you feel angry with yourself for being so gullible;

- The emigration of a close friend or relative whom you miss so much that you can no longer enjoy your social time.

Thirdly, if you know that you are still being affected by some hurt that took place in your past, this book will show you how you can safely revisit these experiences and do the healing that could not be done at the time. The Emotional Healing Strategy has, for example, helped many people recover from many different kinds of old hurts and stop their sabotaging effects on their personality or life choices. Here are some examples:

- Not having had enough unconditional love in childhood which makes it hard for you to maintain good self-belief or to curb your people-pleasing habits;

- An early experience of school bullying that may stop you from standing up firmly enough for your rights or made you into a bully when you reached adulthood;

- An unhappy or difficult childhood that makes you reluctant to have children or is affecting your style of parenting;

- A past betrayal or a bitter divorce that is preventing you from making a commitment to someone you love now;

- A traumatic experience of an illness or a death that has left a legacy of generalized anxiety and fear and makes living life to the full more difficult;

- An abuse of trust by a colleague or old boss that is negatively affecting your ability to work co-operatively with your current team;

- The first- or second-hand experience of the effects of war, ethnic cleansing or a major disaster that you survived but many others did not that has left you with guilt, prejudice or an over-protective attitude towards your family.

As I said earlier, this book has been written partly in response to the many requests I have had from individuals who wanted to know the secret of my personal success in overcoming my own lengthy catalogue of emotional hurts. You will see that I have therefore included much more information about my own hurts than I normally do in my books. However, I have also included many examples of the experiences of other people whose hurts have been very different from my own. So although the majority of my experiences have been within the European culture, colleagues, clients and readers from all over the world have shared their emotional hurts and healing problems with me.

Most emotional hurt appears to produce feelings and repercussions that are universal. Although the individual traumas may appear to be very different in kind, their sufferers often share the same problematic experiences. They commonly find themselves at the mercy of their painful feelings and moving on feels like an impossible challenge. Although, as we shall later discuss, some of the causes of these difficulties may vary from culture to culture and individual to individual, I have found that the general remedial principles of the Strategy seem able to transcend these differences.

So (arrogant as this might sound!), I believe that anyone from any country or background who has the motivation, concentration and self-discipline to work through a self-help programme could find this book useful. In addition I believe many others could benefit indirectly. Excellent role models of emotional resilience are very inspiring and are often keen to support others.

In this day and age, when life moves so fast and we are exposed through the media to such extreme problems, it is easy for our personal hurt to be sidelined or pushed inside by ourselves or by others. As we shall examine later, in the long term this can have a detrimental effect on physical and mental health, and on the potential for achievement and successful relationships. So, in the end, this sidelining of personal hurt can have a negative impact on the wider issues that may seem more important. After all, surely the major problems of the world stand a better chance of being resolved if teams of emotionally balanced and positive people work in harmony to find solutions.

OUTLINE OF THIS BOOK

Before You Begin

This section discusses emotional wounds and why we need to heal from them. You will find out why some people find it harder than others to heal, and how to overcome resistance to healing.

The Emotional Healing Strategy

This section describes how the seven-step strategy and this self-help programme were developed. It explains each of the seven steps including the obstacles which may be encountered at each stage. Exercises, guidelines and suggestions will help you to apply the strategy to a variety of hurts.

Living with the Enduring Hurt

Some residual inner hurt from deep emotional wounds can endure after you have healed well enough to move on. So this section gives suggestions on how you can manage such feelings so that they are less likely to resurface in a destabilizing way.

Helping Others to Heal

Here you will find suggestions to help you use what you have learned from this programme to help others through the healing process. There are also guidelines for helping children, friends, employees, students and fellow citizens whom you may not know well.

HOW TO USE THIS BOOK

I suggest that you first read this book from beginning to end without trying out any of the tips or exercises. As you go along, mark the sections which seem to resonate most with you and note down any memories or thoughts that are triggered.

When you re-read the book, do so very much more slowly. You will need to work through each chapter doing the exercises and trying out some of the suggestions as you go. Initially, even though a current major hurt may be troubling you, I suggest that you experiment first by applying the strategy to a mini-hurt rather than a big one. This will help you to understand the process and see that the step-by-step approach works. There will then be less chance of you becoming stuck at one particular stage when you apply the programme to more serious and problematic hurts.

The book can be adapted easily for use in a self-help group. Such a group would only need a minimum of two people. This may be something that you could do with a friend who is also interested in this subject. Working this way, you can motivate, support and even challenge each other. The strategy is also a useful tool for helping others because its structured approach ensures that the helper doesn't become overwhelmed by personal emotions and keeps the main focus on self-help solutions. But, for the moment, as this is your first reading of the book, I suggest that you 'road-test' the advice first yourself by applying it to your own experiences.

I hope that you find the Strategy and other suggestions in this book help you to build your emotional resilience in the way it has done for me and many others. There is no way we can avoid all emotional hurt, but when it does come, as this wonderful Chinese proverb reminds us, we don't need to let it weigh us down forever.

> You cannot prevent the birds of sadness from flying over your head but you can prevent them from nesting in your hair.

Before You Begin

Why Emotional Healing?

Throughout this book we will be discussing and working on feelings which are generally labelled as 'negative'. But one of the most life-changing lessons I have learned personally is that *all* feelings have a positive function. This knowledge has been crucially important to me. It has helped me to accept and deal with my sadness and anger rather than blot them out of my mind with work or temporarily suppress them with a glass of wine or some other kind of ineffective self-medication.

Emotions evolved in humans as our lives became more complex and we needed to bond together into interdependent societies. They are automatic survival responses. When an event that has relevance to our well-being is perceived, either internally or externally, a set of responses is set in motion which produces changes in our bodies and minds to enable us to make the best of the situation.

It is easy to appreciate the constructive purpose of those feelings which are generally considered to be 'positive'. Love or pleasure on meeting someone we desire revs up our hormonal systems so we are ready for the possibility of procreation. Compassion slows us down: makes us listen to a baby's cry and encourages us into caring action. The excitement that accompanies a great idea stimulates us physiologically so we have energy and motivation to carry it through.

But our so-called negative feelings have important survival jobs to do as well. Let's look at the purpose of some of these:

- **Sadness** slows down or even stuns our systems so that we are inclined to take 'time out'. This means that we can rest and/or run away for protection until we have recovered from the vulnerability and other effects of our loss. It also produces chemicals that induce non-verbal signals such as tears, alerting others to our relatively helpless and weakened state and inducing compassion in them which will stimulate their caring response.

- **Disappointment** works in a similar way to sadness but its responses are in a lower key. Its main purpose is to alert us and others to the fact that we have to slow down and take time to think, as a new direction may be necessary.

- **Embarrassment** shows us that we have been wrong-footed. It generates introspection which could make us aware that we need to learn or brush up a social skill, give an apology or build up more confidence. The anxiety we feel produces non-verbal signals such as blushing and blinking that are intended to appease and generate sympathy in others, which should stop reasonable people taking advantage of our state.

- **Anger** alerts us to a threat. It produces physiological changes in our bodies which will help us to either get away fast or stay and fight. Our hearts beat faster and our breath is more shallow so we have extra energy, and our muscles tense up so we have greater strength. We pant, colour up, shout and clench our fists so others are warned they may need to fight or back off.

An understanding of the positive purpose of such feelings is one of the key foundation stones of good healing. As I will explain later, if we ignore their SOS call for action we can suffer serious repercussions in both the short term and the long term.

WHAT EXACTLY IS AN EMOTIONAL WOUND?

> Just as broken bones may end up stronger than unbroken ones,
> so the experience of grieving can strengthen and bring maturity
> to those who have previously been protected from misfortune.
> Colin Murray Parkes, *Bereavement*

The concept of a 'wound' is most commonly seen in relation to physical damage to living tissue. But we also freely use it as a metaphor for emotional damage as well:

- *'You've hurt me . . . I'm really upset.'*

- *'She really bruised his ego.'*

- *'He cut her with that sharp tongue of his.'*

- *'She is heartbroken – she doesn't know how she can carry on without him.'*

- *'The disappointment really stung – I had been so looking forward to it.'*

- *'I feel absolutely gutted.'*

There is of course a big difference between physical and emotional wounds. The physical kind is visible to the naked eye and can often be felt through touch. You may argue about the seriousness of a physical wound but you would not be able to deny its existence in some form or other. This is not so with emotional wounds. As there is no physical evidence to prove an emotional hurt exists, people often don't believe someone who says they are experiencing one. You must have heard similar conversations to these yourself:

Hurt person: 'He knew turning up late would hurt me.'

Sceptic: 'You can't really be hurt just because he is delayed at work. You're making something out of nothing.'

Hurt person: 'I am gutted about not getting that job. I don't feel like going out tonight.'

Sceptic: 'How can you be gutted? You told me that you had zero chance. Come on, you promised me we'd go to that new bar. You can't back out now.'

Hurt person: 'I'm heartbroken . . . I know we have been at each other's throats for years but I still love her. I don't want a divorce.'

Sceptic: 'You're not heartbroken. Be honest, you just don't want the hassle of a divorce. It suited you to carry on having the affair with Simone.'

However, these feeling-sceptics may soon have to find another subject to argue about. Neuroscientists using advanced imaging scanners can now see and track the physical presence of emotions. They are also able to link the electrical impulses in the brain with the biochemical changes that set off the physical symptoms of feelings that we are aware of. Perhaps in the distant future we may be able carry around a portable scanner which we can use to demonstrate to the sceptics that we are feeling the hurt we say we are feeling!

Maybe it won't be long before science can also offer us a verifiable definition of an emotional wound. As I have chosen to use the term 'emotional wound' throughout this book, you need to understand what I mean. So here is my own definition:

- An emotional wound is a feeling, or a collection of feelings, triggered by an external happening or an imagined happening, which is then perceived as painful by the person experiencing it.

These wounds may not be visible but they are just as real as their physical counterparts. They too need to be protected and healed as quickly and efficiently as possible.

> The greatest mistake in the treatment of diseases is that there are physicians for the body and physicians for the soul, although the two cannot be separated
>
> Plato

WHY IS IT IMPORTANT TO HEAL FROM EMOTIONAL WOUNDS?

Just like the sensations that accompany physical wounds, the sensations that accompany emotional wounds are, as we acknowledged earlier, a warning. They are letting us know that something needs to be done. As with physical hurt, we ignore these warnings at our peril. Sometimes, if the emotional wound is a mere surface scratch (such as a minor put-down), it may heal itself if there is enough emotional oxygen (such as peace and pleasure) in our everyday lives.

But we mustn't forget that even minor wounds – both physical and emotional – use resources and need some time to heal, even if we are not conscious of the process. A collection of minor wounds could, therefore, require the same healing time and energy as one of the more serious and painful ones (such as an unjust criticism or a failure that threatens a relationship or job).

Until the conscious or unconscious healing of a wound is completed, our physical and mental systems are running in a low-powered state. Like a car that is in need of a service, they are not performing at their best. They will not work as efficiently or be as quick or responsive as they are normally. This may not pose a problem while we are cruising down the quiet country lanes of life, but once we take them into the stress of a fast motorway or a congested town they can cause trouble or even break down.

So, if we are carrying around festering emotional wounds while maintaining a low-key lifestyle, we may not feel any significant strain or restraint. But who can guarantee that life will remain stress-free forever? Everyone suffers emotional knocks and these are notorious for happening when we least expect them. Furthermore, we sometimes find ourselves flying out of the frying pan and into the fire of a knock-on problem, or yet another hurt.

Most people are aware of how important it is to heal from relatively serious emotional hurts, but few give enough or any attention to the smaller hurts. It is standard practice in most societies, for example, to make allowances for those who are recovering from close family bereavements and to give help to victims of major crimes and large-scale disasters. Most developed societies even fund professional counselling or voluntary services specifically designed to help people recover their emotional equilibrium after such events.

Lesser hurts rarely receive the same kind of acknowledgement. This is true even for some events that may be generally accepted as traumatic. Redundancy is one example. It often causes multiple losses, personal relationship problems and severe wounding to self-respect. But the type of counselling that might be allocated rarely covers emotional healing needs. Instead, it encourages immediate focus on the positive work or opportunities for the future. Even if the emotional hurt is acknowledged by the employer or counsellor, individuals are usually expected to deal with this aspect of recovery themselves.

But amongst all the other tasks unemployed people have to do, it isn't surprising that emotional healing rarely assumes priority. They are usually overwhelmed by the desperate desire to secure their next job immediately. So feelings of anger, sadness, fear and possibly shame are pushed deep inside and left to fester. These may later emerge as irritability at home, or cynicism or inhibiting anxiety in their next job.

Similarly, no employer is likely to give you compassionate leave to deal with the sudden loss of a best friend. In today's world of family breakdown and estrangement, this might be a much more significant wound than the loss, long-expected, of an elderly parent. How many people have you heard saying they are taking time out to help themselves recover from this kind of deep loss? The most that people are usually able to do is attend a funeral service. Perhaps those who are lucky enough to have a creative talent or an appropriate profession may also, as I have done, dedicate one of their works to them.

The price you might pay for not attending to small wounds (as well as the more obviously serious ones) can usually be seen in a number of areas in your life. Let's take a specific look at some of these . . .

Happiness and Fulfilment

> Only a man who has felt ultimate despair is capable of feeling ultimate bliss.
>
> Alexandre Dumas

When we regularly depress the emotional pedal on painful feelings, we dampen down our sensitivity to emotions generally. (A general flattening of emotional responsiveness is one of the key symptoms of the serious mental illness we call Depression.) This means that while we are harbouring inner sorrow or anger, our potential to feel joy, excitement and positive passion is also being restrained.

Even if we have no major problems or setbacks to deal with we may settle into a kind of second-best life. In fact, it is this effect that often prompts clients to seek my help. It is common for people to start their first session by saying something similar to the following examples:

> *'I'm not even sure why I am here. I haven't got any big problems like so many other people. I have a reasonable job and a good marriage, but I just never seem to feel excited about anything any more. I just feel as if I am drifting through life. Perhaps that's just the way it is as you get older . . .'*

'It was my girlfriend's idea for me to come and see you. She's convinced there is something wrong with me. She says she has a feeling that I'm not happy – even though I keep telling her I'm fine. I think I'm just a low reactor. I don't get passionate about anything. That's me. She's got this idea that because I never have anything to do with my family any more, maybe there is something that happened in my childhood. I know it wasn't the best, but then lots of people have had to put up with worse . . . My dad left home when I was six, Mum just got on with it and she soon remarried anyway. I didn't get on with my stepdad and that's the main reason I don't see them, because we just used to end up arguing. I don't miss them.'

In my experience, this symptom of flattened positive feeling can almost always be traced back to one or more unhealed wounds. If the original hurt was some time ago, it can take a long time to both uncover and heal it. To make matters more difficult, the habit of flattening positive feelings has frequently become integrated into the personality and affected their expectations and behaviour in other respects. The people who exhibit these traits may even think that their unemotional style of being and living is 'normal'. Because of the 'like attracts like' principle, they are surrounded by similarly apathetic people at work and in their community. Sometimes they convince themselves that their comparatively dull style is superior. They will give examples of the problems which 'hysterical' or 'wild' types bring upon themselves when they have their fun. They will also frequently argue that life is tough and most of the time just has to be endured. They will even try to get me to agree to this, by reminding me of the disasters, divorce rates, endless violence and of course death by various means that confront us daily through the media. In short, they have lost their faith in happiness, which to my mind is one of the most tragic losses of all.

She knew by now his extreme sensitiveness, for which his acid irony was a protection, and how quickly he could close his heart if his feelings were hurt.

Somerset Maugham, *Painted Veil*

This kind of happiness deprivation also has many other knock-on negative effects, as research into the roots of happiness at the University of California clearly indicates. They discovered that the primary components of a happy life such as positive feelings, emotional intelligence and strong social bonds are deeply inter-twined. Experiencing and expressing positive emotion is at the heart of almost all kinds of love. Positive emotions can contribute to the growth of new skills and competencies; negative emotions often undermine growth.

Another important study was done by Dr Alice Isen from Cornell University in the USA. She found that even mild happiness improved performance because it made people think differently. They were more able to consider a problem from all angles, so they had a better chance of coming up with solutions. This means we may underachieve in terms of our potential at school and at work.

So, by suppressing the feelings and memories of unhealed emotional wounds we are giving up on our potential to be as happy and successful as we can be. If we make a habit of doing this, a vicious downwards cycle can develop:

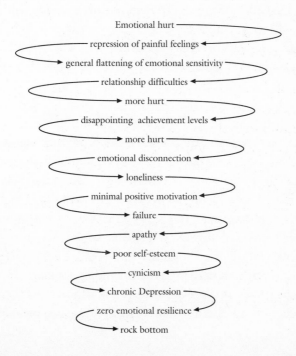

Emotional hurt
repression of painful feelings
general flattening of emotional sensitivity
relationship difficulties
more hurt
disappointing achievement levels
more hurt
emotional disconnection
loneliness
minimal positive motivation
failure
apathy
poor self-esteem
cynicism
chronic Depression
zero emotional resilience
rock bottom

Perhaps this illustration may seem like an over-dramatization of the problem. But to anyone who has been a psychiatric patient, a Samaritan or has worked in a pyschiatric hospital, it will certainly appear very familiar.

Remember that the further down the cycle you are, the less consciously aware of your problem you become, and the less able you are to help yourself. As someone who has personally experienced this frightening phenomenon, I know that I will never knowingly take the risk of doing so ever again.

Health

The link between emotional health and physical health is now so generally established that you don't need an extra warning from me. Most of us, for example, have probably read at least one article in the popular press or seen programmes on television that have linked repression of anger to high blood pressure, digestive disorders and muscular aches and pains. Those of us who have suffered the effects of major grief know only too well how deeply sorrow affects the immune system. We know that it makes us more vulnerable to viral infections. Research also indicates that a prolonged state of grief can exacerbate more serious conditions such as cancer and heart disease.

As a result of research into the links between physical and emotional health, the growth of integrative medicine is on the increase. And we can expect even faster growth in the next few years as interest in this area is now escalating. The University of Wisconsin is to open a multi-million-dollar institute specifically for research into the relationship between the emotions and physical health. It will have state-of-the-art MRI brain scanners to track emotional ups and downs in patients while monitoring their health over a long period of time.

But substantial though this kind of funding for emotional healing programmes as a preventative physical health measure may be, I believe it is a distant dream in many countries, including my own. So I guess that the ball is likely to remain firmly in the court of the individual for many years. Anyone who has experienced emotional hurt doesn't need more proof that it can affect their physical health and their will to look after themselves. We have felt the tension in our muscles and inside our heads; the sickness in our stomachs; the flutters of our hearts; perhaps experienced the urge to drink more alcohol than we should or the lack of motivation to eat well, exercise or even to clean our teeth.

Finally, let's not forget the impact of unhealed wounds on our mental health and indeed on the mental health of the people who live and work with those who suffer from such wounds. Depression is not the only potential knock-on mental illness that can develop as a result of emotional wounding. From my experience in working with people with a wide range of mental health symptoms, I am convinced that unhealed wounds (sometimes from as far back as childhood) are also frequently a root cause of phobic, compulsive and addictive illnesses.

The stress of any form of mental disorder on others around the wounded person can then lead to mental health problems for them as well.

World /Community Relations

> Wars, through destruction and self-destruction, afford the ultimate opportunity to finally rid ourselves of the emotional pressure built up in us since childhood
> Alice Miller, *Breaking Down the Wall of Silence*

One of the greatest influences in my own research into emotional wounding was the Polish psychoanalyst and philosopher Alice Miller. Miller claims that the repressed feelings of childhood abuse brought about the cold, calculating, destructive and violent natures of dictators such as Hitler and Ceausescu. This made a deep and lasting impression on me. Of course, I am well aware that there are many other factors as well which can, and do, have a bearing on the development of ego-centricity, heartlessness and cruelty. But Alice Miller's work, together with that of British analyst Anthony Storr (author of *Human Aggression*), made me much more aware of the macro implications of unhealed emotional hurt.

Furthermore, I am convinced that emotional healing makes people more caring towards others. When emotionally upset clients first come to see me, they are often self-obsessed. As they heal, I watch them become more outwardly focussed. The state of the world, the politics of peace and current stories about atrocities and disasters begin to enter into our discussions. Although I always wait until the client brings up such subjects themselves, as long as they are sufficiently healed, I am more than willing to gently encourage their interest. As you will see later in this book, Step Six of the Emotional Healing Strategy is called Channelling. At this stage, when the main recovery work has been done, some extra healing can be derived from using the urge that emerges quite spontaneously to engage in some action which will help others.

> Because we have suffered an emotional trauma, we can speak out because we know what it is like to feel vulnerable and are filled with a longing to protect others
>
> > Frances Lawrence on UK Human Rights legislation, [the widow of Philip Lawrence, a head teacher who was murdered by a 15-year-old boy in 1995 outside his school.]

Emotional healing is far from being the cure-all for the wider problems which we now face in our modern world, but I do believe that it can empower and motivate individuals to make a positive and constructive contribution to their communities. The depressed, bitter, cynical, vengeful, selfish and obsessive behaviour that festering emotional wounds can foster is certainly not conducive to the maintenance of a peaceful, mutually caring community.

WHY DO SOME PEOPLE FIND EMOTIONAL HEALING EASY AND OTHERS FIND IT HARD?

Emotional healing appears to me to be a natural survival response. Very young children don't ignore their hurts. They scream for help and attention. Their parents then respond instinctively and give them the healing they need. Their children learn the healing habit by copying this behaviour and practising their art on their teddies, dolls, pets and their parents!

But, of course, like any other instinctive survival learning process, this one can also be interrupted or completely blocked. Throughout the book, I shall be addressing why this may happen at certain stages, but it might be helpful now to briefly look at some of the most common saboteurs. As an example, I will share with you how these corrupted my own education in healing. I hope this will help prompt you to think about how you may have been personally affected by similar factors.

Poor, or Nil, Role-Modelling

We all know that perfect parenting rarely occurs. Some of us may not have had the kind of parent or caregiver who had the inclination, time or skill to heal us and help us practise and develop the habit of healing ourselves. Perhaps they were too wounded themselves to be able to help us.

My father certainly was. He had unhealed wounds dating back to his childhood and many other traumatic wounds from his adult life buried inside him. (They didn't surface until he had a very serious, prolonged breakdown at the age of 70.) My mother was, according to people who knew her, a natural healer. She was apparently a brilliant nurse and it is interesting that my father fell for her while she was nursing him. But she became an alcoholic during my infancy and was unable to care for her children in any way. My siblings and I spent most of our childhood in local authority childrens' homes, looked after by parent-figures who had neither time or patience to deal with tears or tantrums in a healing manner.

Macro-Cultural Influences

In some cultures, emotional healing is nationally and openly recognized as an important need. Emotions are respected and there are rituals and channels in place which encourage the safe expression of sadness and anger. People are given the space, comfort and other support to help them recover before returning to their ordinary everyday lives.

In other countries and communities, it may be culturally unacceptable to do this. It is considered a sign of strength and/or holiness to be able to 'button up' and 'soldier on' in spite of what you may be feeling inside. Rewards in the education system may be highly slanted towards achievement in highly disciplined rational thinking.

I was born and raised in the UK, a country that is generally considered to be the birthplace of the 'stiff upper lip' . As I was born in the midst of war, this national trait was understandably even more pronounced. I was raised and educated in relatively secluded and austere convents where martyrdom was lauded and happiness was expected in the after-life rather than in the present. I learned to harbour an (undeniably comforting) inner belief that the more suffering I tolerated, the holier I would become. I am sure it is no coincidence that, as an adult, when I was still healing, I was drawn towards southern Spain where emotions are generally much more openly expressed, comfort is given freely, even to strangers in emotional distress, and religious rituals and fiestas go hand in hand.

Micro-Cultural Influences

Examples of these are our dominant education system, work environments and social circles. Some jobs, professions and forms of education require people to keep their emotional hurt within themselves, or it has become established practice to do so. Examples of these are the armed forces, the emergency services, professions that demand predominantly rational thinking such as accountancy, pharmacy, IT, science and highly academic research.

In other areas it may be generally more acceptable and normal to display and deal with emotion, at least amongst your fellow students and colleagues. Examples of these might be specialist music schools, art colleges, medical auxiliary work, counselling, acting, art, teaching and marketing. Hobbies of this ilk are amateur dramatics, playing music and singing; boxing, rugby or dancing.

In spite of the likelihood that I was genetically disposed towards rational thinking, it is, once again, no coincidence that emotional neediness in my early adulthood drew me towards the theatre and the helping professions and into a bohemian social life full of artists. I was particularly attracted to those who lauded emotional pain, seeing it as part of life's rich experience of both darkness and light.

WHEN IS THE BEST TIME TO HEAL AN EMOTIONAL WOUND?

Now! Seriously, the answer to this question is always the sooner the better. It is much easier to work through the strategy if you begin as soon as possible after the hurt has occurred. It is easier to recall what happened. You have quicker access to the emotions because they will not have had time to be repressed and, if the hurt is very recent, you may still be physiologically affected.

Equally, though, it is never too late. I have seen people success-fully heal from their childhood emotional wounds much later in life, in some cases well past their retirement. In fact, this may often be a very good time to embark upon this healing, with time and space to spare. But I would not advise waiting that long if at all possible. After all, we have seen the damage that unhealed wounds can do.

I am aware that we are very often so busy in life coping with the crises caused by hurt, that emotional healing has to be post-poned. In this case, the general rule is to do it as soon as you are able to make adequate time to give it the attention which it deserves. After reading this book you should have an idea of how long each wound will need. However, healing is not an exact science, it is an art. You must be prepared to be flexible.

Introducing the Strategy

> The failure to recognize the impact of minor losses is one reason
> why people are often so poorly prepared when a major loss occurs.
>
> Bob Deits, *Life After Loss*

The seeds of this self-help strategy were planted many years ago.
I 'discovered' this simple natural process while working with a
group. In order to help a client to understand why she felt better
at the end of our session and what she still needed to do in order
to complete her recovery, I told a story. It was about how some
good parents helped their child heal emotionally from an everyday
disappointment. I will recount this simple story now because I
believe that it is still a good illustration of emotional healing done
simply and naturally.

Six-year-old Ben had spent weeks looking forward to going
with his mum (Rachel) and his dad (Simon) to a theme park.
On the day they were due to go, Simon received an early-
morning call from his boss. There was a serious emergency that
only Simon, a hospital maintenance engineer, could deal with.

When Ben woke up, Rachel broke the news to him that their
day out would have to be postponed. He started shouting and
stamping his foot and saying things like, '. . . But you promised.
You shouldn't break promises.' In response, she tried to give
him a hug but was pushed away, so she calmly repeated what she
had said before: 'I know we promised because we never thought
this would happen. But things have changed and Daddy has just
had to go to work. We are really sorry. We didn't want to let you
down and we know you must be very disappointed.'

Later, when she noticed that he had gone into one of his quiet moods, she encouraged him to talk about what had happened and what he was feeling. She helped him to articulate the mixture of feelings of disappointment and anger that were whirling around inside him. He then broke down and started sobbing. Rachel cuddled and held him securely until he calmed down. She then said, 'We must try and think of something nice to do today instead.' She suggested various options and Ben chose to go with her to see his grandma whose cat had just had kittens. He spent an enjoyable day being spoiled and playing with the kittens.

When Simon arrived home in the evening, he explained to Ben that his colleague, who was supposed to be on emergency duty, was ill so he had to go in to repair an important machine at the hospital. He said that he was sure Ben would understand how important it was to do this as it might be a matter of life and death for someone, while they could easily go to the theme park on another day. Ben said, 'Okay . . . when can we go?' A date was arranged and Ben started to tell Dad about the kittens.

After telling this story, I summarized the steps that Simon and Rachel had taken to help Ben heal from this relatively small emotional hurt. I put the key words of each on to a flip chart and highlighted how their behaviour could be contrasted with less helpful ways of handling the situation. Below is an outline of this analysis. I have highlighted the names which I gave the key steps and put the 'not-so-healing' parenting approaches in brackets. (The latter may ring some bells for you, as they did with the people in the group that I was working with. Sadly, most adults who find emotional healing difficult were probably not lucky enough to have parents who tended to respond to their children's hurts in the effective way that Rachel and Simon did.)

Rachel:

- Encouraged Ben to **explore** his hurt – what had happened and what he felt, by talking about it (rather

than maybe being relieved that he seemed to have
forgotten about it and using the peace of his quiet
mood to busy herself with jobs);

- Allowed him to **express** his feelings (rather than
perhaps saying he shouldn't be that upset and to
think about his poor dad having to work and the
poor people in hospital);

- Gave him **comfort** with a cuddle (rather than maybe
telling him, 'No, now that's enough – big boys don't
cry over such little things. I thought you wanted to
be a brave fireman when you grow up');

- Encouraged him to think of a **compensation** for
himself (rather than perhaps telling him he was lucky
to be fit and well enough to go to the theme park
another day, and that lots of children in the hospital
would never be able to do that).

Simon then continued to help Ben to heal by giving him some
additional comfort and also helping him:

- To gain some **perspective** on his hurt by seeing his
experience in a wider context (rather than perhaps
by ignoring it and asking about grandma and the
kittens, and being relieved that his wife had dealt
with the emotional fall-out from his emergency
call-out).

After doing this simple analysis, we agreed that Ben's parents'
actions had enabled Ben to put this hurt well and truly behind
him, and that it was highly unlikely that he would have feelings
of resentment lingering inside him.

We then went on to look at how Ben could have become
super-healed if two further steps had been taken. First, his parents
could have:

- Encouraged him to **channel** the learning he had
  gained from this experience constructively. For
  example, if his kid sister had faced a similar
  disappointment, they could have reminded him
  about his experience and encouraged him to comfort
  his sister and find some compensation for her.

Secondly, his father could have:

- Made Ben feel even better by saying he was sorry and
  asking for his **forgiveness**.

So because Simon and Rachel were naturally good parents, they
helped Ben, equally naturally, to heal by taking him through the
first five essential stages of the Emotional Healing Strategy,
Exploration, Expression, Comfort, Compensation and Perspective.

Later, Ben might have become super-healed if they were then
to have taken him through the last two bonus stages: Channelling
and Forgiveness.

Of course, Ben's hurt was fairly trivial in the grand scheme of
life's disappointments and challenges, and it may not, in some
people's opinion, have merited super-healing. What his parents
did was quite enough to enable him to move on happily. But if
they had taken these two extra steps, not only would he have had
some bonus healing, but both his sister and his father might have
benefited as well.

The telling of this story and our analysis of the step-by-step
healing process proved to be so enlightening to everyone in the
group that fortunately I saved that piece of flip chart paper. If I
hadn't done so, perhaps I might never have remembered this
helpful 'theory' that had emerged somewhat magically from my
subconscious mind.

By this time in my career, through my training together with
my own experience of recovering from hurt and my professional
work as a therapist, I had amassed a vast amount of wisdom. So
it wasn't really magic, it was simply my right brain doing a bit of

useful sorting and chunking together all this stored information. What was so helpful about this seven-step analysis was its simplicity. I knew that this meant that, if it truly could be applied to a wide range of both minor and major hurts, it had great potential as a self-help tool.

Over the ensuing years, I tested it out on myself, on my friends and on my clients. This simple theory became such an invaluable therapeutic tool that I developed it into a practical strategy. I used the same seven words that had been on the flip chart as the names of its seven steps. I included an outline of these steps in two previous books, *Self-Esteem* and *Emotional Confidence*. But it is only now, after fifteen years of trial and error, that it has finally matured and become sturdy enough to form the heart of a self-help programme in its own right.

I am aware that you may have already heard about other stage-by-stage models for dealing with the recovery process from emotional hurt. In particular there are two classic ones which I know that many people have found useful. The first is the Dr Kübler-Ross Grief Cycle:

Denial ➤ Anger ➤ Bargaining ➤ Depression ➤ Acceptance

This model is widely used in grief counselling.

The second is the Lewis-Parker Transition Curve:

Immobilization ➤ Denial ➤ Incompetence ➤
Acceptance of reality ➤ Testing ➤ Search for meaning ➤ Integration

This model is widely used in redundancy and change management programmes.

The Emotional Healing Strategy, like both the Kübler-Ross and Lewis-Parker models, provides the hurt person with a comforting rational explanation for their emotional turmoil. It gives them hope and a sense of security because it also anchors them somewhere in a known step-by-step process of recovery. But this Emotional Healing Strategy has some different and additional aspects. First, it is a multi-purpose model that can be applied to almost any kind of emotional hurt. Secondly, it divides the healing process into two stages: five essential and two non-essential ones. Thirdly, it offers practical guidance on recuperative action that the hurt person can take, because it is designed as a self-help tool rather than just as a theory for understanding the healing process.

OUTLINE OF THE STRATEGY

As I have already indicated, there are seven steps in total. The first five are the essential ones in the strategy and the last two are non-essential 'bonus' steps that could help you to become super-healed. The bonus steps are not appropriate or necessary for every emotional wound. If you complete the first five steps, you will be healed sufficiently well to move on with your life. Your hurt will not feel like a hindrance and your feelings will be under your control.

Here is an outline summary of what you will need to do at each stage.

The Five Essential Healing Steps

1. *Exploration*
   Acknowledge and examine the hurt.

2. *Expression*
   Allow yourself to experience, at least to some small degree, the physiological sensation of the feelings and express them safely and appropriately.

3. *Comfort*
   Be emotionally soothed by receiving caring attention either from yourself or from someone else.

4. *Compensation*
   Receive or give yourself some kind of recompense.

5. *Perspective*
   Gain some understanding of how and why the hurt
   occurred and assess its true significance for the 'big
   picture' in terms of your life.

Bonus Healing Steps

6. *Channelling*
   Find a constructive outlet for using the benefits and/
   or learning from the experience of the hurt.

7. *Forgiveness*
   Find a way to 'wipe the slate clean' and move on
   without any residue of negative emotions in relation
   to the person or persons who triggered the hurt
   feelings.

Using the first letters of each of the headings, I devised a
mnemonic sentence to help in memorizing the steps and their
order. It can also double as a motivational statement that you can
repeat to yourself if the going should get tough.

EVERY EMOTIONAL CUT CAN PRODUCE CREATIVE FRUIT

The order in which each of these steps is placed in the strategy is
crucially important. The strategy is based on what appears to be
a natural step-by-step process. Once one stage is satisfactorily
completed the urge to move on to the next one should arise quite
spontaneously. When it is working automatically (as it does for
some lucky people such as Ben's parents) there may not appear
to be any clear dividing line between the stages and indeed there
can be an overlap between them. But for those of us who have
to learn or relearn how to heal, it is more helpful to see the

stages as quite separate. Most of the healing problems I have encountered are due to one or more of these factors:

- **Hurrying too fast through the stages** so that there is not enough time for them to work. (This could be due to cultural or personal pressures to get back to business. Healing can be postponed. It is better to do this than to do it inefficiently. It could also be due to the fact that you might still have some resistance to truly healing. We shall be looking at how to deal with this in the next chapter.)

- **Skipping certain stages** because they appear irrelevant or are too uncomfortable. (There are some common underlying reasons why this happens which we will address as we deal with each step later in the book.)

- **Becoming stuck in a stage** because another unhealed wound has been resuscitated. The original wound may then need healing attention before you can move on. But more often than not it can just be acknowledged and a plan made to deal with it later. I suggest you use one of my own psychological tricks:
    Imagine that you have a 'Personal Development Shelf' at the side of you. The idea is that, in your mind's eye, you watch yourself physically placing the 'issue' which needs your attention on the shelf while telling yourself that you will deal with it later. Like many of these kinds of tricks, it sounds odd but it works!

OVERCOMING ANY RESISTANCE TO WORKING ON THE STRATEGY

'I seem to be coping much better now, thank you. I'd rather not dig up the past unless I need to do so. I'll just see how it goes for a while.'

'I haven't thought about it for over a week now. You seem to have done a miracle cure already. I'm so busy right now that I'd rather keep going while I can. So I'll come back to you later if it returns to haunt me.'

These are the kinds of comments I have often heard just as someone is due to start working on this strategy. So although you have been motivated enough to pick up this book, you may find your enthusiasm on the wane at the start of the next chapter! If this happens, rest assured that you will not be alone. At the thought of reviving painful past trauma, it is natural for your psychological system to kick in automatically and protect you. Its way of doing this is to set in motion a defence mechanism which psychologists call 'Denial'. This is the brain's response to severe psychological pain. It pushes images and memories down into our subconscious so effectively that we become genuinely convinced that we no longer have a problem and are not in need of any kind of help.

In a recent radio interview, I heard Rush Limbaugh, a top US talk-show host with a 20 million+ audience, recall his experience of denial. It came after he received the diagnosis of a condition that was causing a very rapid loss of hearing. Obviously this was particularly devastating news for him as his highly successful career was threatened. He recounted how listeners were starting to comment that he was taking longer than usual to answer questions. This was indeed true, because he was already needing to have the questions transcribed before he could answer them. But rather than admitting that the pauses were caused by his hearing loss, he instead blamed the electronic advertising system the station was using. He was in denial about his deafness. At some stage later he accepted and faced his problem. Then he was able to have a state-of-the-art electronic device fitted into his ear. This enabled him to carry on with his show and recover his psychological equilibrium as well. As a result, he has become a highly effective champion for emotional healing as well as disability causes.

Denial has to be convincing. This is because in the immediate aftermath of a hurt it may be essential to get into action. Rush Limbaugh, after his devastating news, had a radio show that needed to go on air. Similarly, after a mugging, we may need to contact the police or secure medical help. After bereavement, there may be funerals to arrange, wills to be dealt with, children who need food and dogs to walk. Should we be made redundant, we may need to work 'coolly' on, in order to secure a good reference or a loan to tide us over. In such situations denial can be helpful, and can even be life-saving, because it has the power to transform an emotional wreck into a resourceful coper in seconds.

However, like so many other useful pain-relieving quick fixes, denial can become addictive and habitual. Indeed it can become entrenched within a personality pattern. You may well have come across 'tough-skinned' people who never seem to experience emotional hurt at all. If you have been tempted to envy them, don't! A suppressed emotional pedal flattens feelings indiscriminately. As a result, these 'buttoned-up' people usually miss out on pleasurable feelings as well as the painful ones. Indeed they often approach me in the first instance not for help with their emotional wound, but because they have lost their ability to feel deep joy, love and passion. Commonly they have become depressed or their ability to feel and express positive emotion has affected an important relationship.

So, when we have been emotionally wounded we must be always on our guard for denial. But this is much easier to say than to do. Denial is so difficult to spot in ourselves. If we are lucky, a perceptive friend or relative may notice what has happened. Sandy, who had been recently jilted by her boyfriend of eighteen months, recalled being brought back to conscious reality by her mum who said to her:

> *'You may feel fine but you're not. I saw the tears beginning to well up when Margaret mentioned his name last night. And you've got deep shadows under your eyes. You're not getting enough sleep and you have lost a lot of weight too quickly. You have to stop pretending you're okay and deal with it now.'*

Sandy was lucky. Can you guarantee that someone will always do the same for you? However much you are loved, people around you may be too busy to notice, too timid to confront you, or simply too sad themselves to want to see your tears or anger. This is why I am suggesting you play safe and take the following precautionary action.

Safety Precautions to Deal with Denial

1. Appoint a caring but assertive friend or relative as your 'healing monitor'. Ask them to enquire about your progress at specified intervals such as once a week or once a month. Brief them about your favourite excuses and the rationalizations you may come up with (e.g. 'I've just been too busy'; 'My back's been playing up'; 'I've not thought about it all this week so I must be getting better anyway').
2. Make a list of the reasons why emotional healing is important to you. Write them out on a card and display them somewhere you will see them regularly.
3. Set a date for starting the strategy now and let your monitor know! Then, reward yourself for having the courage to do both!

Dealing with Complex Resistance

Unfortunately, although denial is the most common saboteur you will encounter at this stage, there are others. Negative thinking, low self-worth, embarrassment, shame and lack of energy can also cause resistance. Sometimes a number of these will surface together. When this happens it becomes harder to give general advice. You will see from the following stories springing from similar hurts that the resistance needed to be dealt with in different ways.

Jane and Tanya were students at the same university. Both encountered unfair treatment which left them with emotional wounds that were affecting their academic progress as well as causing other problems. Both these young women were seriously sceptical about the relevance of Emotional Healing to their issues. You will notice that although Jane's resistance was somewhat complex, her blocks could be dealt with relatively easily. Tanya's, on the other hand, required much more time and help from a professional.

Jane's Story

Jane was studying to become a pharmacist. In her second year at university she was wrongly accused of cheating over a project. It was argued that the work was well above her usual standard and it was implied that she might have had too much help from her uncle, whom her tutor knew to be a pharmacist. As the accusation was difficult to prove or disprove, Jane was forced to agree to take a lower grade for this piece of work. She was understandably annoyed about the incident. Her family advised her to put the experience behind her and move on. They said that this was life and could happen to anyone. They argued that it was an understandable mistake, because Jane had worked particularly hard on this project and, as a result, it was of higher quality than her previous work. What was most important, they said, was that Jane knew she was in the right and she just had to prove her innocence by keeping up to this standard.

But this was exactly what Jane found she couldn't do. Why? Because (as is often the case) her suppressed anger turned into a depression which affected both her motivation and her concentration. She refused counselling at the university and instead started to look at other less academic career options.

The previous year, I had successfully helped her older sister with a change of career direction, so Jane came to see me. However, after our first session, I was not convinced that she needed to change course. The root cause of her problem was not a mistaken choice of career; it was the unhealed hurt from the cheating accusation. Although Jane took some initial persuading, she did eventually agree with my diagnosis.

Jane's main defensive arguments against taking the emotional healing approach, which I have listed below, were very familiar. I'd be surprised if you haven't used one or two yourself sometimes. I certainly have. Below each I have summarized the action we took to deal with these. As you can see, we used simple self-help strategies. If this book had been written at the time, my services as a therapist would have been redundant!

Resistance Block 1: There are plenty of other easier and less upsetting options.
Jane: 'What's the point in getting upset again? A job is a job. There are plenty more career options.'
Action: Reality reminders. We looked at the length of time that she had been dreaming of becoming a pharmacist. She could date this back to having her first chemistry set at nine years old. Her dream was then frequently tested out by doing holiday jobs in her uncle's pharmacy. We also reviewed her natural aptitudes and personality strengths. This confirmed what she already knew – that she was ideally suited to this career.

Resistance Block 2: Other people have to deal with much bigger problems than mine.

Jane: 'My parents think I should be able to just forget it and move on. They have had much worse to cope with in their lives.'

Action: We examined the difference between her and her parents' personalities and the differences in their cultural backgrounds. She reinforced her right to be an individual with different needs by repeatedly saying the following affirmation: *I am different from my parents and can choose my own solutions to my problems.*

We then also reinforced her right to heal from small emotional wounds by reminding her of the price she could pay in terms of health and success by not doing so.

Resistance Block 3: There's nothing wrong with me. I just need . . .

Jane: 'I'm not sick – I just need career advice.'

Action: I gave her a leaflet on depression from the charity Depression Alliance which described her symptoms almost exactly.

Resistance Block 4: I'm a hopeless case and I was born that way.

Jane: 'They're right, I should just have the courage to face the fact that I'm too thick and lazy to make the grade.'

Action: We reviewed her history of academic achievements, which indicated that she was above average in innate ability and perseverance. She acknowledged that her most recent grades were unusually low. She admitted that her drop in standards coincided with the start of the hectic social life that she threw herself into after the incident.

After overcoming these blocks of resistance, Jane successfully worked through the Emotional Healing Strategy and is now a qualified pharmacist. Undoubtedly it was to her advantage that, prior to this incident; she had been in good psychological shape. Her self-belief was high and she did not have a past history of similar hurt to complicate her problem.

Tanya's Story

Tanya's wall of resistance was much harder to break through. It is doubtful whether she would have acknowledged her need for emotional healing without the ongoing support of a coun-sellor or therapist. Nine months previously, she started to develop a close friendship with Daniel, a senior male lecturer at her university. He had shown a particular interest in her research project and offered her some extra-curricular time to discuss it. As a result of these meetings a mutual physical attrac-tion developed. When Tanya refused to let the relationship become sexual, this inappropriate 'social' relationship began to cool.

A number of weeks later Tanya learned that Daniel had started a relationship with a fellow colleague. In a fit of jealous rage, she lodged an official complaint of sexual harassment. The university authorities decided not to take any action against the lecturer because a) there was no real evidence to back up Tanya's story, and b) her classmates had jointly sent a letter to the Registrar which challenged the accusation and praised Daniel's professionalism. However, Daniel was disturbed enough himself by the incident to look for another job in a neighbouring university.

Once he had left, Tanya started to regret her hasty vengeful action. She was shunned by other students for 'forcing' their most popular lecturer to leave. But even more importantly, she missed Daniel and began to feel utterly heartbroken. Against her own better judgement, she started to stalk him. She bom-barded him with pleading texts and daily letters which he bounced back unopened. Finally, she visited his new place of work and followed him around. This prompted a sharp warning letter from Daniel's lawyer which, she said, 'brought me back to my senses'. To help push her feelings and memories into the back of her mind, she then threw herself headlong into a lively (and promiscuous) social life.

However, the story of Tanya's hurt didn't end there. She began to develop an unsightly skin rash which was attributed to stress by a dermatologist. She scoffed at this diagnosis because she said she was perfectly happy, having lots of fun and was not stressed about anything. It was only the threat of permanent scarring that made her agree to have a few sessions with me.

Tanya's lack of motivation was a serious stumbling block for some time. She was convinced that there was nothing wrong with her and appeared to be determined to prove that this was so. It was not until our penultimate session that she finally revealed an important earlier incident that was undoubtedly highly significant.

At the age of fourteen, while on an exchange home visit in France, an older man had made inappropriate sexual advances towards her. At first, this man, her pen-friend's father, had been particularly welcoming and generous. He showed great interest in her French art project and went out of his way to take her to exhibitions and galleries. However, one day he started to play 'footsy' with her under the family dining table. Inwardly, she was highly embarrassed and upset. Outwardly, you would never have guessed there was a problem. She put on a 'cool' front and ignored his behaviour. From then on Monsieur became increasingly 'very busy' and Tanya recalled having to endure whispered jibes from him for the rest of her stay. Tears welled in her eyes when she was asked if she had discussed the incident with anyone. She hadn't felt she could even tell her sister because she felt so ashamed. Indeed, it became clear that she still felt that way. She blamed herself because 'He probably thought I was leading him on. Dad was always telling me that I dressed indecently.'

So, Tanya had previously not only experienced a serious abuse of trust at an impressionable age from a father figure, she had also damaged her self-esteem by blaming herself for it. Furthermore, she had an even more serious hurt to deal with in regard to her relationship with her father. After this incident she shut herself off emotionally from him and still hardly ever saw him. As she had been the apple of his eye until she reached puberty, this was a severe loss.

So no wonder Tanya's denial of her emotional pain from the recent incident at university was so strong. This particular wound to her self-esteem had rekindled these two much more serious festering hurts from father figures at an impressionable age.

Before being able to use the strategy to heal from these three emotional wounds, Tanya needed another programme of sessions with me to rebuild her battered self-esteem and motivation. Eventually she was able to put each one of these experiences well and truly behind her. Like Jane, she too was then able to get back down to her academic work and complete her degree. She is currently exploring the world with her boyfriend before starting a training contract with a law firm. Her career choice may well prove to be a useful of way of channelling the hurts from her injustices. If so, she would then be naturally moving on to the first bonus stage of healing (Step Six of Emotional Healing Strategy – Channelling).

I hope Jane and Tanya's stories have illustrated how crucial it is to look out for resistance and take action to deal with it rather than put it off indefinitely or abandon your healing work. My tips for denial or the kind of steps that Jane took will be sufficient to deal with most blocks. But if you find that after taking this kind of action you still have a problem, don't forget Tanya's story. You may need some professional help (or a perceptive friend) to help you 'dig' a little deeper to uncover the root causes of your resistance. Above all, trust that there is always a 'good' reason why you may be putting off doing the healing that you need to do. Some time in the past your psychological system will have 'judged' (rightly or wrongly) that it was necessary to protect you from the pain of a hurt. But now you no longer need that protection, you have a strategy for healing which in the long term will prove to be much more beneficial to your health and well-being.

> Nothing fixes a thing so intensely in the memory as the wish to forget it.
>
> Michel de Montaigne

The Emotional
Healing Strategy

1. Exploration

This first step in emotional healing is to explore the exact nature of your hurt with a view to reviving your past and present experience of the hurt. To do this you will need to recall as vividly as possible your memory of what happened and the context in which it was happening. As we discussed in the previous chapter, this is rarely a task that any of us welcomes, but hopefully you are now motivated enough to give it a go so that you can move on.

If the incident happened very recently and is quite minor in terms of emotional hurt, this will be a relatively easy task. In these kinds of situations you may already do this quite naturally and spontaneously by talking through hurtful incidents with friends or family. The following example of how I did this recently with the help of my husband illustrates this. You will note that I have highlighted the words which indicate that I was engaged in Exploration even though I was unaware that I was doing so at the time.

A few weeks ago, I had a frustrating call while I was on a bus. It was from the accounts department of my phone company about a bill that was supposedly outstanding. I knew this bill had been paid but the person who rang kept insisting that this was not the case. His tone was abrupt and haughty as he informed me that, as there was no record of it having been paid, arrangements had been made to disconnect my number within the next few days. He said that I had the option to pay it immediately by credit card and then if I could prove that I had already paid, I could apply for a refund. This was tempting to do as I was going to Spain the next day but I refused. Instead I asked to be put through to the supervisor. He was reluctant to do this, but eventually agreed to transfer me. I hung on the phone for ten minutes listening to irritating music and messages informing me that I was in a queue. I was then cut off. I spent the rest of the journey trying to get back in contact with the person who had rung me. The moment I arrived home, I **recounted** the whole saga to my husband. He listened patiently as **I told him how it had left me feeling frustrated and angry.**

So, in a couple of seconds, the Exploration of my hurt was over and done with. Thanks to my long-suffering husband, I had reviewed my recall of what had happened and I had identified the emotions that the hurt had triggered. You can probably recall occasions when you have done this kind of natural exploration many times yourself and listened to others while they did the same.

However, although Exploration is a natural response after a hurt, it doesn't always happen quite so easily, as it did for me on this occasion. Very often it is postponed because we need or choose to divert our attention to other matters. If this happens, the task can become more difficult. First, we may be reluctant to bring back the memory. Secondly, we may not be able to recall the incident so clearly. But even with these obstacles in the way, it often still takes place without making any conscious effort. This is especially true if there is a curious and caring person around who will prompt and encourage the exploration. As my husband has both these character traits, I often have the benefit of his unsolicited help! To illustrate how this can happen, let's imagine a different (but equally possible) ending to my story.

Let's suppose that after my upsetting call I arrive home and notice that my husband is looking tired and stressed. Instead of talking through my frustrating experience, I begin to ask him about his day. He tells me that he has had a horrendously difficult journey home and very heavy meetings all day. I listen and encourage him to talk. As we are about to sit down with a comforting cup of tea, a client rings. She has encountered a serious problem which she talks about briefly. I go to my office to look at my diary and offer her an appointment. When I return to the sitting room, my husband is watching the news on TV. Together we observe with horror graphic film footage of another suicide bombing and then yet another distressed parent whose child has gone missing.

Understandably, the memory of my frustrating encounter with the phone company disappears into the recesses of my mind. However, the next day it is revived. En route to the airport, I open a letter from the phone company confirming that I am about to be disconnected. My husband hears me give a big sigh and sees me shake my head. He asks me what the letter is about. I reply irritably, 'You don't want to hear! I'll just get in a bad mood. It's not that important and we are running late. You have to concentrate on driving.'

On the plane, my persistent spouse brings up the subject of the letter again. **He encourages me to talk about what happened** the previous day. As I find it **difficult to recall** the details, he **helps me out by asking questions and making comments.** Doing this **jogs my memory and revives the feelings of hurt.**

In this imaginary ending to the story of exploring this mini-hurt, you can see that the task could also have been done some time after the event quite naturally. But, because it had been delayed and become overshadowed by other life events, it was not quite such an easy process. The highlighted text illustrates that this belated exploration needed to be prompted into action. In my fantasy example I was encouraged by my husband, but in our real busy world this kind of spontaneous help is not always so readily available. We cannot depend on the caring attention of others. We may have to prompt ourselves or *ask* for encouragement from a specially selected person.

So let's assume that you have overcome any lurking resistance and are ready to start the exploration process. Here's some advice about how to cope with the common difficulties you could encounter.

FOCUS ON WHAT AND NOT WHY

It is quite common to find yourself wandering off the Exploration path. Your task here is to examine your recall of WHAT happened. Very often two unhelpful WHY habits make us veer in the wrong direction. The first is to start trying to analyse why the incident happened. For example, returning to my mini-hurt story, I might have been tempted off track by talking about the depersonalization of customer service since the arrival of sophisticated telephone call handling systems and computerized billing. If I had done this I would have been jumping forward to Step Five: Perspective.

The second common diverting habit is to try to understand why you felt what you felt. For example, I could well have started to blame my own pre-holiday stress for causing me to become overly upset about such a minor everyday frustration. If I had done this I would have been trying to jump even further to Step Seven: Forgiveness.

To help keep yourself on the true Exploration track, try prompting yourself with the kinds of questions you will find in this next practice exercise:

Exercise: Exploring a Hurt

Think about a relatively small hurt that you have experienced in the past and Explore it by answering the relevant questions below.

- What sort of day was it?

- What do I recall seeing?

- What do I recall hearing?

  What do I recall saying?

- What did I notice feeling then?

- What do I wish had happened?

- What do I wish had not happened?

- What was I disappointed about?

- What did I lose?

- What do I miss?

- What have been the consequences of this hurt?

- What do I feel now?

- What was especially hurtful about what happened?

DON'T EXPECT PERFECT RECALL

That which touches the heart is engraved in the memory.

Voltaire

When doing your Exploration you may find it difficult to recall some details of the surrounding hurt even though you still have vivid flashbacks of the emotional highlights. Let's briefly explore some of the relevant knowledge we have to date on this subject:

- Memories are recorded more or less strongly depending on how emotionally laden and personally significant the event is to *us*. Voltaire and many others knew this fact years ago, before science could observe this phenomenon in action.

- Our mood at the time of the event also affects the way we record it. Positive life events tend to be remembered slightly better than negative ones. We are also more likely to remember a broader picture of the event.

- The more an event is recalled and recounted the more firmly it will be fixed in our memory. So if you have buried the experience of your hurt inside you, it will not be stored quite as firmly as those that you may have shared many times with others.

- If we are very frightened or angry, our brain focuses on certain objects, sounds or smells and the other surrounding aspects of the event may not be noticed or recorded in our memory. This is because our brain is engaged in storing a blueprint version of the event so that if we meet the 'danger' again our brain can instantly and automatically take protective action to prepare us to cope. So, we may be able to recall only certain 'highlights' rather than details of hurts that were very frightening and very frustrating.

- Memory function improves if we sleep well. Often during the time of an emotional hurt and immediately after it, our sleep is disturbed or even non-existent.

- Our memories are not static. They change over time. Each time we recall something we restructure the memory according to what has happened to us since and how we are now. As unhealed hurts tend to make us depressed over time, we may find it harder and harder to recall any of their positive aspects. This means that the memory is likely to become even more negative.

Let's look at how this all works in action.

For the purpose of quick reference and easy explanation, I call the brain's ordinary processing of everyday emotionally neutral or low-voltage events 'The Wisdom Way'. The route this process takes in humans goes through our cognitive thinking centres. Here the event is analysed so that an appropriate feeling and action response can be consciously chosen.

The other kind of processing which I referred to earlier is used for events with high emotional content which the brain considers to be emergencies. I call this 'The Jungle Speedway'. This route by-passes the cognitive centres and is not given a rational analysis. Instead, it is sent immediately to a more primitive response centre in the brain. Here the event is unconsciously and instantly matched with a pre-conditioned protective response. This is either a basic Fight/Flight/Freeze reaction or one that has been pre-programmed into us in our childhood or through our experiences of major traumas.

In reality these processes are two ends of a spectrum. Many events do, of course, fall into a category in between the two so the emotional response and its effect on the memory is often processed in part by The Wisdom Way and in part by The Jungle Speedway. The following are examples of the two extremes but they will give you an idea of how differently hurtful triggers can be processed and imprinted on our memories. You will see that I have summarized the end result, including its effect on our memory.

The Wisdom Way in Action

You had a pleasant relaxing evening and slept well last night. On your way to work, you hold a door open for a mother struggling to get through with a pushchair and two hyperactive toddlers. The mother doesn't even look at you to say thank you or smile or nod. Furthermore, she just jerks her son away without an apology as his ice cream splashes all over your coat.

- Analysis of the situation in the brain's cognitive centre: 'She is so stressed and preoccupied she didn't mean to be rude. Forget the incident. At least you had a good night's sleep.'

- Brain's instructions to the body: dry up the tear ducts, deepen the breathing, relax the muscles.

- Action: shrug your shoulders and walk on.

- Effect on memory: the setting and event will be recorded in detail.

- Follow-on effect: in the long term this event is unlikely to be remembered, unless you are heavily prompted to do so.

The Jungle Speedway in Action

The same event occurs, but on this occasion you are in a hurry because you overslept as a result of being up half the night arguing with your partner. In this stressed situation you perceive the event as being the 'last straw'. You think that your best coat has been wilfully covered with ice cream by someone who didn't care a damn about you when you were only trying to help them.

- The primitive Fight/Flight/Freeze emotional processor's response: search for an Emergency Blueprint. Find a match for 'Ignorant Insult'.

- Brain's instructions: fill eyes with tears, bow head (for protection), put up hands to cover face and muffle crying (to avoid inviting further insult). Run away and hide. Produce hormones to fix highlights of the incident firmly in your memory.

- Effect on memory: when you try to go to sleep that night you have flashbacks of that insensitive mother's face and that sticky white mass descending on you. When you tell your partner why you are tired the next day, she or he asks questions such as, 'Was she young?' 'What nationality was she?' or 'Were the kids boys or girls?' You say you haven't a clue because all you can remember is that revolting ice cream coming towards you.

- Follow-on effect: the next time you see any woman with two kids and a pushchair coming towards you, you get another flashback and you automatically turn and run in the other direction. Every time you retell the story to someone who is mystified by your behaviour you dramatize it a little more until it really does fit better with your original negative thought that the 'attack' was wilful.

Here are some other brief examples of emotional memory in action in hurtful situations. Perhaps you have encountered a similar one yourself. If so it is likely that you would have remembered:

- The raised voice and criticism of your boss and not her praise for certain aspects of your work or her suggestions for improvement;

- The glaring eyes of a person attacking you, but not the colour of his hair or what he was wearing;

- The open door through which you can make a fast exit, but nothing about the building or anyone else around;

- A disclosure of infidelity from your partner, but not how often it occurred or who it was with;

- The exam grades you failed, but not the grades which earned distinctions.

The police and lawyers are only too aware of this recall difficulty when people are emotionally upset. They are continually working with victims of crime and accidents whose recall is crucial, but however honest the person may be, their story is often frustratingly inconsistent with the factual evidence.

Therapists working with people who have been seriously hurt or abused by someone they loved in their childhood frequently encounter this problem. Sometimes the memory of highly hurtful events may have been completely obliterated. It is fairly common knowledge nowadays that survivors of sexual abuse often have nil recall. I was made especially aware of this phenomenon when I was invited by a paediatrician to witness a special examination at a hospital. A ten-year-old girl had been exhibiting a range of sexual abuse symptoms since she was four years old. The most serious of these was that she would wake regularly during the night screaming in pain, desperately calling out in a very young voice, 'Mummy, Mummy' for about 30 minutes, and clutching her vagina and anus alternately. She was obviously in a state of terror but was impossible to comfort. She would get angry when anyone tried to ask her about her pain. In the morning she would have no recall of the nocturnal dramas.

During the examination she was given an injection of 'truth-revealing' drugs which took her into a hypnotic state and induced flashbacks and a major recurrence of her pains and terror. All of the twelve people present, including the police and many other highly experienced professionals, were convinced that she had regressed to about four years of age and that she had re-experienced a sexual abuse trauma. However, on being woken she still had no recall. Fortunately, though, there was enough circumstantial evidence for the courts to stop her from having any contact with her father, whom we were all convinced was the abuser. These particular symptoms then ceased but she remained emotionally very fragile and suffered severe attacks of depression. I later learned that during one of her low periods at the age of eighteen the memories of the abuse finally began to surface.

Thankfully very few people will have such a serious trauma to heal from. But even smaller hurts can cause a similar repression of memories. This is more likely to happen if they occurred in early childhood and were often repeated. Interestingly, research has shown that the person's relationship with their primary care-giver can have an effect on recall. The more secure it was the better chance they have of recalling such memories. These findings were particularly interesting for me. They explained why I had so little recall of my own early childhood.

When I first started having therapy after a suicide attempt in my early 20s, I found that I had virtually no memories before I was ten years old. My brain had suppressed both the good and the bad. I had to ask other people for the story of my childhood. This was not an easy task as I came from a British stiff-upper-lipped family, whose shameful skeletons were always locked firmly away. But I did find out that my parents constantly quarrelled from my conception onwards; that my mother was seriously alcoholic and often neglected us. From time to time she would become so out of control that we were taken into care. The series of children's homes in which I spent the majority of my childhood were not like the ones I see today. They were understaffed and overcrowded with poorly trained staff. I certainly did not have any kind of quality relationship with a 'primary care-giver'.

If I had not been encouraged to explore my personal history after my suicide attempt, I would not have realized that my problems had any link to being emotionally hurt as a child. I would have continued to think that my 'faults' were intrinsic to me and my personality and could not be corrected. After this exploration I began at last to feel and express the sadness, anger and envy that I had had to suppress for so long. I was then able to move out of my self-punitive rut and continue working through the rest of my healing journey. An interesting bonus of this process was that a number of happy memories from childhood did return. However, I am still only able to recall very few of the bad ones.

So don't be dismayed or discouraged if you cannot recall every detail of what happened to you or the context. Remind yourself that you are not in the dock or acting as a witness to a crime scene. Your task is to heal you and your hurt and it is possible to do that, as I have done, with only minimum recall. Your memory of the 'true facts' does not have to be perfect. Later on in your healing journey when you reach Perspective, you can, if you wish to do so, gather more factual information. In this final essential stage, finding out what actually happened could be very helpful. But for now, all you need to do is recall enough to enable you to make contact with the feelings your hurt triggered.

FOCUS ON *YOUR* PERCEPTION OF WHAT HAPPENED

It is also important when you are working in this stage of Exploration to remember that it is *your* perception and interpretation of what happened that matters. You are recalling what you believe hurt you or, as in a case like my own, what you think is likely to have hurt you. This is also why other people's views on the hurtfulness of the experience are neither relevant nor necessary.

Indeed, other witnesses' views of what was hurtful or what was not can sometimes be counterproductive. If they contradict your own interpretation, you may begin to doubt your right to the feelings you need to. make contact with in order to heal. The following story about Tracey may help you to understand why this is so. You will note that she and her sister Bryony recalled the same event in their childhood in very different ways. This is because their individual beliefs, their position in the family and the information they had had previously affected their perception. Their story also illustrates how different the emotional legacy of the same hurtful event can be for each person.

Tracey's Story

Tracey consulted me in an effort to understand why she was always breaking off relationships just when she was beginning to get close to the other person. This was happening not just with the men in her life, but also with girlfriends. She was particularly angry with herself for 'picking a fight unnecessarily' with her latest boyfriend. She felt he had been a perfect match for her and so she was in despair about herself as well as broken-hearted.

In the process of exploring possible root causes of her problem, Tracey told me that she and her sister had been deserted by their mother and brought up by her father and later a stepmother. At the time her mother left, Tracey was six. She recalled (honestly, I believe) that her mother '. . . just suddenly ran out of the house and was never seen again. Dad said that she had gone to live with her boyfriend.'

Tracey herself suggested that her sister Bryony should come along to speak to me at the start of one of our sessions as she had a much better memory of their childhood than she did.

Bryony, who was two years older, was quite angry when she heard what Tracey had told me. She said: 'You know full well that Mum said where she was going and why she had to go. She didn't have any choice . . . and anyway, I don't know why you are making a fuss. You didn't care. You just carried on playing. It was me who had all the problems. I had to look after you when Dad was too drunk to do so. And you could do no wrong when Deidre [their stepmother] came on the scene'.

Interestingly, the sisters had not talked about these matters before. They were indeed very different in personality, but still very fond of each other. A kind of unconscious 'contract' had been established between them up until this time not to talk about their childhood. Both had understandably wanted to put it well and truly behind them. This is not uncommon. Many siblings do this. My brother and I did not discuss our painful experiences in the children's homes until we reached adulthood.

In terms of Tracey's healing, all that mattered at this stage was that she recalled her own perception of what happened. Her sister's perception was interesting (particularly to me as the therapist) but unhelpful. Indeed, as the result of hearing her sister's interpretation Tracey felt worse not better. It began to reinforce her belief that it was something about her own make-up rather than her traumatic background that was at the root of her problems. This was making her even more resistant to healing the hurt of her mother's departure. If I hadn't intervened to remind her that it was her memory of the event that mattered, she would not have acknowledged and later expressed her feelings of terror when she was 'abandoned' by her mother.

Not surprisingly, Bryony also had problems, but her emotional experience and her emotional wounds were different. Hers centred on anger (starting with her father whom she witnessed being violent towards her mother), but she did not think there was any point in talking about the past or her temper ('That's just the way I am'). Any hope of an exploration of her hurts was being blocked by the common problem we have already discussed of searching for the 'Why' around her hurt.

So remember, you can use other witnesses' recall to jog your memory. But it is your perception of what happened and your feelings that you need to clarify while you are Exploring. In the Perspective stage, other's people beliefs, experiences and opinions can be very useful. So don't argue and fall out with your witnesses over 'the real truth'. Just thank them if they offer their side of the story and tell them you would like to talk more about it later.

FIND THE WORDS TO DESCRIBE YOUR FEELINGS

'Words can't describe how I feel.'

Only last week I found myself uttering this phrase to my daughter after receiving a major let-down from someone I had trusted and valued. Fortunately, my psychological internal warning system started flashing immediately! It was telling me that I needed to do some Exploration. My emotions were in turmoil and out of my control. I was feeling several different emotions so deeply that I was overwhelmed. In this state, I knew that I (along with any other human being) could not act rationally and make good decisions. I also knew that, until I moved from this position, I could never heal from this emotional wound.

Exploring feelings and hurt through language helps switch the focus of our brain's activity from its primitively programmed emotional centres to those in the cortex region which houses our more sophisticated thinking department. (More on this subject in the next chapter.) Once we have found words to describe our feelings, we immediately begin to feel a little better. This is because we are more in control. We will have regained a sense of our personal power and balance because we are thinking as well as feeling. We can now analyse, plan and know which particular feelings need attention in our next stage, Expression.

It is also extremely helpful to find specific adjectives to describe **the degree of each feeling** you have. This does not, of course, have to be an exact measurement. But knowing, for example, whether we are 'slightly angry' or 'very angry' is very helpful when planning the application of the rest of the strategy. So if you find yourself with no words to describe your state, try some of these suggestions.

SUGGESTIONS FOR ENCOURAGING EXPLORATION

Use Memory Prompts

Gather a collection of memory joggers from your archives. These could include, for example, the following:

- Photos

- Newspaper or magazine cuttings

- CDs (or LPs!)

- Bric-a-brac

- Clothes

- Books, files and letters

- Food and drink

Set aside some time to sit silently amongst these. Pick up each in turn and complete the sentence 'This reminds me of . . .'

Talk Face-to-Face with Someone Else

You can do this with a good friend. It doesn't have to be someone who knows anything about what happened or any of the people involved. It just needs to be someone you can trust to keep what you say confidential and who is a good 'active' listener. This is the kind of listener who encourages *you* to talk as opposed to the kind who just chats or sits more or less in silence as you talk. In my chapter on helping others to heal there are some tips on helpful listening. You could always show these to your friend if they are getting it wrong for you. If they would be offended by you doing this, they are not the right person to be helping you with this task. (Remember that doesn't mean they are not still a good friend and perhaps could help you at some other healing stage.)

If you are worried about imposing on someone, just make it easy for them to refuse by saying that you would not mind at all if they couldn't help and that you would easily be able to get someone else if they couldn't or didn't want to for some reason.

If you do not have such a friend, find a voluntary or paid counsellor or therapist to talk to. Even though you may think that you have had an extraordinary experience, nowadays there are self-help groups or specialists in almost all areas of emotional hurt. A search on the internet or an enquiry at your library or health clinic will find the contact details of relevant national organizations. These should be able to direct you to someone locally who could help.

Remember that just because someone is a trained counsellor they may not give you the kind of help that you want without being told what that is. So tell them what you are doing and specifically ask them to help you explore and recall what happened. If you find your sessions with them are not helpful, have the courage to say so because they may well be able to change tack. (I know that I have many different styles of working with clients and often have to experiment a little before finding one that suits.)

If you have had a very major childhood hurt, I would always advise that you start your Exploration by talking to someone rather than by any of the other means that have been suggested.

Talk on the Telephone

Sometimes it just isn't possible to find someone to talk with face-to-face, so you could do the same task as above by ringing a friend. But do not immediately launch into talking about your hurt, as many would then find it difficult to tell you if it was not convenient to talk at that moment. This is, after all, the kind of call that needs the listener's full attention and a private location from which to talk.

Instead, explain that there is a personal problem that you would like to talk through and it would need at least ten to fifteen minutes of their time. Ask them when it would be convenient to ring them back.

Start this pre-arranged call by immediately explaining what you need (forget the small talk). Then give them an easy way of saying no as I suggested above. By doing this you will ensure you get the quality committed attention you need and deserve.

If you prefer to talk anonymously to a stranger, you could use one of the many help-lines that are now available. The numbers for these can be found using the same suggestions as I gave earlier.

Talk Electronically

The Samaritans, one of Britain's largest support organizations, have been running an email version of their confidential phone line since 1994. They now receive around 300 messages a day via the web. A spokeswoman recently said:

> *'A lot of people find it hard to talk about their feelings in confidence,' says Samaritans' counsellor Sarah Nelson. 'Many of them find it easier to write it down. The majority of our email seems to be from younger people – perhaps because email offers a space that's not available on the phone. They can say words which they may never have spoken out loud, and email really allows them to express their feelings. People seem to be able to speak about more severe problems more openly.'*

Other self-help organizations are now following suit. Many other people are also using internet chat-rooms and blogging sites for this purpose. But if you choose to do this, take very great care about disclosing the fact that you feel emotionally hurt (and therefore more vulnerable) unless you are on a very secure and well-monitored site.

Write

Write letters and emails to people who have shared the experience, but who may have a clearer memory of what happened. (But remember what we said earlier – that it is your perception that counts at this stage of your healing.)

Another popular way to begin to share a hurt is to write a letter to a magazine or newspaper 'Agony Aunt'. Whilst this is not the best source of help for your Exploration task, some may give you suggestions of organizations that could be of assistance.

Finally, you could just try writing in private for only yourself to read. I often suggest to clients that they buy a notebook specifically for this purpose that is small enough to carry around with them. Thoughts and memories often spring into our minds 'out-of-the-blue'. Noting these down can help you stay in control of your feelings and you can look at them later when you have time and are ready to do some Exploration.

You can also use the book just to write down a stream of consciousness. Knowing that no one else is listening or will read them may help you to explore aspects of the hurt that you would not otherwise have done (e.g. giving a 'voice' to thoughts which you find shameful or embarrassing).

Finally, a brief word of warning about publishing any writing you do at this stage. There is currently a vogue for 'hard-luck' autobiographical books. But don't be tempted to rush into publishing your account of a hurt before you have fully healed. You may find that the knock-on effects of doing this can be too hot to handle.

In his book *The Kid Moves On* Kevin Lewis talks about this phenomenon. He unlocked major emotional distress during his continuing Exploration of his childhood abuse with the media and the public when his first book *The Kid* became a best-seller. To deal with the flashbacks and feelings he started drinking heavily, over-eating and trying to control his emotions with obsessive ritualistic behaviour.

> I had no idea how to handle these difficult emotions. I was in danger of drowning and was clinging to my life of bad habits like life-rafts . . . it was a pattern from my past that I thought I would never be repeating, but I didn't seem to be able to stop myself.
>
> Kevin Lewis, *The Kid Moves On*

Imagine

Research on memory has revealed that it is much easier to recall something in the context in which it happened. This is why in Dramatherapy groups we try to recreate the scene by using props and rearranging the furniture. If you are Exploring on your own, you can use your imagination to recreate the scenario. But don't do this if your hurt has been a deeply traumatic one (and many that are difficult to remember are). There is no point in retraumatizing yourself. You don't need to do this in order to heal, even if you are working with a therapist.

Use Art

Some people find it easier to start the Exploration process without using words at all. If you think this might be the case for you, use coloured pens or paint to 'dump' images and/or symbols of your hurt on to a large piece of paper (you don't *have to* fill the sheet!).

Alternatively you can create a 'sculpture'. This is a collection of objects selected and arranged to represent your hurt.

With either method, be careful not to judge what you are doing by any artistic standards. This could get in the way of the spontaneity you need when you are trying to Explore memories which might be in your subconscious.

When you have finished, Explore further by just pointing to areas of your 'work' while saying one word that comes into your head. Be careful not to start making intellectual interpretations. If you (or anyone else) does this, there is a danger that you will distance yourself from your feelings. The main aim of Exploration is to generate contact with authentic feelings that your hurt has triggered, so that you can move forwards and Express them in our next healing stage.

EXPLORATION IN A NUTSHELL

The purpose of Exploration is to recall the memory of what happened and what you felt without worrying about:

- Whether your memory is perfectly correct or not;

- Anyone else's version of events;

- Who or what may be to blame;

- The seriousness or otherwise of the hurt.

2. Expression

Your aim in this stage is to experience the feelings that are associated with your hurt and allow yourself to Express them to a certain degree.

Perhaps you already started to do this as you were exploring your wound. But equally you may not. There is no right or wrong in any of our various reactions to similar circumstances. Human beings differ tremendously in the way that they handle feelings. This becomes very obvious when you witness a group of people undergoing the same trauma.

A few months ago, three managers were referred to an outplacement consultant whom I know. They had all been told that their jobs were at risk by the same person using the same prepared speech.

For all of them the news came as a complete shock. They each had an excellent track record and had good reason to be optimistic about their future with the company. They were all in their thirties, had young families and similar heavy financial commitments. The previous week they had attended a meeting with their director where they discussed their strategies and budgets and were told that the company was in good shape and the forecast for the coming year was encouraging. Their differing emotional reactions to the bad news were noted by the Human Resources Manager.

1. Marco stormed out. He said he was furious and went straight away to demand support from his professional association representative.

2. Gill smiled and shrugged her shoulders. In response to being asked how she felt, she said she didn't think

there was any point in getting upset. She added that this could have happened to anyone, anytime, and you just have to find a way to get on with it.

3. Jim said nothing and his face was impassive. When he was asked how he felt he said, 'I don't know – I still can't believe it.' A close colleague commented that she thought he was 'gutted', because he had become very quiet and was obviously finding it very difficult to concentrate on his work.

Three weeks later, when they were seen by their outplacement consultant, they were all more or less still in the same emotional states. Marco was still openly angry with the company and still set in his determination to 'fight' the decision. Gill was carrying on cheerfully, and said that she was looking forward to her outplacement sessions because redundancy might turn out to be the best thing that ever happened to her. Jim hadn't even discussed the matter with his wife and there were indications that he was drinking a good deal more than normal.

As I don't know these individuals personally, I cannot be sure why they all handled this trauma in such different ways. But let's play a guessing game. This will help to illustrate the main factors which influence our habits in relation to emotional expression.

Why Do Some of Us Express Feelings More Easily than Others?

1. Nature, through our genetic inheritance and biological make-up, predetermines our default temperament.

Marco, as his name suggests, has a good deal of Italian blood running through his veins. This would have made him more naturally inclined to express his frustration and anger more openly than his two colleagues. Their traditional British 'stiff upper lip' emotional style is common amongst northern European races. It became a much-talked-about phenomenon when Princess Diana died. Our royal role models maintained an outer reserve and hid away while their emotions were at their rawest. In contrast, in Spain, where I live much of the time, feelings are expected to be much more openly expressed. When the Spanish royal family experience a personal tragedy they can be seen reacting very differently. The TV and newspapers tend to be full of images of the family weeping and looking dishevelled and distressed.

But, even if Marco hadn't been of Italian stock, his own individual biochemical make-up may have predisposed him to have quick-firing emotional responses. He could have been endowed with an above average supply of testosterone which would have made him more likely to externalize his feelings of anger so he could fight off the threat. In contrast, Jim could well have inherited a trait which rendered him more likely to develop the illness of depression.

2. Some auto-emotional responses are programmed into our brains as a result of the influences of our early nurturing, role-modelling and cultural pressures.

I know only too well how the influence of nature is often overridden by nurture. Cultural, religious, gender and family conditioning all played their part in taming my expressive temperament. Like Marco, nature endowed me with a quick temper. However, I was brought up in England where, as we have discussed, openly expressing emotions is not considered socially acceptable. In addition, my upbringing further reinforced the suppression of negative feelings. In the children's homes in which I spent most of my childhood it was certainly not 'safe' to express any level of frustration or anger. Being a Catholic and educated in convents meant that I also had a heavy threat of divine punishment.

Jim may also have received severe disapproval for crying when young. But being a boy, he wouldn't have smiled instead of expressing his anger or sadness. Although in recent years, this practice of plugging up male tears has been seriously challenged, men are still less likely than women to be openly expressive. The men who currently consult me on healing issues generally tend to have more of a problem at this stage of the strategy. Many do what Jim did. They adopt the common British male habit of gritting their teeth and using 'the silent treatment' to express their feelings to others. Like Jim, many use alcohol as a suppressant. Others will use playing or watching sport to discharge or divert pent-up emotion.

3. Personal circumstances

The individual circumstances of our lives can also affect the way we habitually express emotions. Our personal situations and our health help influence our default emotional style which can have a predetermining effect on our emotional responses. Let's imagine that, as the result of an unplanned teenage pregnancy Jim has been locked in a loveless marriage for fifteen years. Perhaps Jim was born as a result of a similar mistake on the part of his mother. So when she expected him to do the 'right thing' by his girlfriend, Jim might have felt a debt to his mother who had silently martyred herself for him. This could have caused him to resign himself to passively accepting blows that were delivered by 'fate'.

Marco on the other hand might have spent some of his early adulthood working on a factory floor while he was educating himself at university. He might have become involved in Union politics as strikes were then a common phenomenon. This might have influenced the way he expressed his angry feelings by threatening action from his professional union.

Gill could have recently fallen in love and been inwardly considering the option of leaving work to devote some years to bringing up the family she dreamed about. If so, that could explain her *laissez-faire* style for handling this emotionally charged experience. Taking our fantasy even further, Gill could be diabetic and therefore would need to take extra care not to get upset for fear that doing so might prompt a hypoglycaemic attack.

*

Being aware of the auto-responses that affect our expression of feelings is crucial for managing this stage of healing. We need to know which feelings are genuinely our own and are appropriate and which are simply auto-responses. If the latter are not the same as our own **authentic** emotional reaction, we need to take action to control them. We can do this by using one of the techniques on the following pages. As you become more experienced in handling your feelings this may not be necessary. You will learn to spot the auto-responses. Reminding yourself of where they originated is usually enough to switch off the unwanted feelings. Then you will be free to encourage the expression of your genuine feelings. So here is an exercise that will help to make you more aware of your emotional pre-programming in relation to the expression of emotions.

Instant Exercise: My Auto-Expression Patterns

1. Spend some time generally thinking about the influences that nature, nurture and your current personal circumstances may have on your expression. Answering the following questions will help you to do this, but you may need to ask your family and close friends for information if you have difficulty in answering.

● Was I considered to be a 'cry-baby' or the opposite? Did I cry readily in front of people or did I tend to be a child who cried in bed at night or ran away to hide when I felt sad?

● How did the most significant parent figures in my childhood react to hurt? Did they maintain a stiff upper lip or did they cry or show anger freely and easily?

● Which relative did my family say I was most like? (This could have been a relative you didn't even know.) Do you know anything about that person's emotional expression?

- Does my religion have any strong views or established rituals on handling grief, setbacks and injustice that affect my expression?

- In the country I was brought up in, what is considered to be the most socially unacceptable way to express emotional hurt?

- When I have had a bad day and am feeling tired or very stressed, do I tend to 'go quiet' or am I more likely to cry or get angry and irritable when something goes wrong?

- If I hear some unexpected bad news, do I immediately feel stunned and speechless or would my emotions be more likely to spill straight out in words or action?

- Can people generally spot my true feelings from the look on my face or what I am doing with my body when I am upset? Or are they often surprised when I tell them what I am feeling? If it is the latter, what gave them the wrong impression?

- Am I currently suffering from any physical condition which is likely to affect the way in which I express hurt?

- In the culture in which I live, are boys and girls expected to behave differently?

- In my role at work, am I free to express feelings reasonably openly or am I expected to keep the lid on them?

2. Review your answers with a view to highlighting any habitual patterns of emotional expression that have emerged.

3. Complete the following sentences:

When I feel disappointed I am most likely to express or restrain my feelings by:

_____

When I experience a loss or I am sad for another reason, I am most likely to express or restrain my emotions by:

_____

When I have been hurt by an injustice, I am most likely to express or restrain my emotions by:

_____

THE DANGERS OF NOT EXPRESSING OUR HURT FEELINGS

When a feeling has been triggered by an emotional stimulus, a physiological chain reaction starts even before we are aware that we have that feeling. This response is designed to be a temporary fix with the physical release of feelings ending its emergency crisis response cycle. Let's remind ourselves of a few things that could go wrong if we do not allow the response to complete its natural course.

Our health will suffer if we stay functioning in this physiological mode. Our system needs to get back to its normal functioning state as soon as possible. While in crisis mode our systems do not perform their homeostatic and general maintenance work. The chemicals produced will turn toxic – this could have repercussions on our digestive system and our muscles and organs will suffer under the strain of being driven in top gear for too long. If this emergency state continues for a prolonged period, our immune system will suffer and we will get into further unnecessary physical trouble.

But of course our livelihoods and our relationships can also pay a hefty price. If the internal stress on our bodies mounts to 'bursting point', there is a danger that the uncontrollable amount of emotion will express itself at the slightest provocation. This could prove to be destructive in many ways. You may find your pent-up feeling bursting through at an innocent party or in the wrong place. The consequences of the following two scenarios are unusually severe, but I am sure that you can think of more everyday examples of the same process happening in situations which you have witnessed.

- A boss, who earlier that morning swallowed down his anger at his teenage son's disrespectful and selfish behaviour, then bites the head off a good young employee simply because of a minor transgression that is usually overlooked and treated as normal office practice.
  ➤ The boss does not forget the incident because he feels ashamed. But instead of apologizing he covers up his embarrassment by finding more holes to pick in this person's work.
  ➤ The disgruntled and justly resentful employee leaves. A few weeks later, he is overheard backbiting about his boss's emotional instability at a networking event which a close golf partner of the boss's CEO happens to be attending.

- Paula is heartbroken at the break up of a relationship with a long-term boyfriend, but she is determined to show him and the rest of world that she doesn't care.
  ➤ She stifles her tears, destroys all the photos of him and puts a block on his telephone number and that of his friends. She then sets about having a long series of short meaningless 'flings' with men who are a 'completely different type'.
  ➤ A couple of years later she is asked by her best friend to be her chief bridesmaid. On seeing her friend in her dress and looking so happy, she suddenly feels gutted. She cannot hold back her

years of repressed tears. She feels mortified by her
behaviour. She knows that it is spoiling the best day
of her friend's life, and yet she cannot control her
tears enough to be able to walk into church with her.

HOW MUCH EMOTION DO WE NEED TO EXPRESS?

During the last 20 years my own opinions on this subject have
changed considerably. I now believe that, for the purposes of
healing hurt, you only need to feel and express feelings in the
early stages of their physiological growth. This would mean for
example:

- If you were frightened, it would be enough to feel
  butterflies starting to flutter in your stomach or to
  experience a slight tremor rather than feel a
  full-blown attack of panic with heart palpitations.

- If you were disappointed, it would be enough to feel
  tears welling in your eyes rather than crying your
  heart out.

- If you were angry, it would be enough to find
  yourself gritting your teeth, or clenching your
  stomach or fist rather than shouting out or throwing
  something.

You may have encountered different opinions on this subject, so
let me explain how I have arrived at this conclusion. During my
early career there was a 'fashion' for the kind of therapy that
produced grand catharsis. I was trained in Psychodrama, Dramatherapy and Gestalt, and loved this style of working. We used all
kinds of techniques to encourage people to scream and shout, or
hit cushions representing those who had hurt them. Sessions were
often judged as effective or not by the depth of distress that had

been witnessed and the volume of tears that had been shed. The highly emotionally charged atmosphere was exciting and seductive. Like many others, I personally found this way of working a refreshing alternative to the lengthy talk therapies that I had previously been trained to use. Participants gained instant relief from the release of pent-up feelings and would leave sessions feeling on top of the world. However, over the years I became increasingly aware that there were some down-sides to using this kind of highly cathartic work as a regular healing tool.

First, for safety reasons, these kinds of cathartic sessions had to be supervised by a highly trained and experienced therapist. It takes a good deal of confidence, skill and experience to establish boundaries and keep emotions from escalating out of control. Therapists of this stature can be hard to find and hard to pay for as well!

Secondly, cathartic work is noisy work. It therefore requires space that is private and sound-proofed. This is a challenge to find, especially in our overcrowded British Isles.

Thirdly, it became clear that many people (particularly the most vulnerable) found that their mood took a deep dive when they returned to their more mundane, or difficult, less supported real life. This sometimes caused dependence on this kind of cathartic 'fix'. Many became what were commonly called 'therapy junkies'. When repeated 'doses' of this kind of therapy could not be found or afforded, I witnessed many turning to alternative 'fixes' such as legal or illegal drugs.

At the same time as I was beginning to experience these concerns, I had begun to write self-help books. For these I needed to develop and test strategies that could be used either unsupervised by a reader or by people with a basic level of counselling training. It was while testing out this Emotional Healing Strategy that I discovered (much to my own surprise) that for most hurts, minimal expression of the feeling seemed to work just as well as a major cathartic release. I also found that it was much easier for people to integrate this gentler 'low-voltage' kind of healing work into their everyday lives. This meant that many more people could benefit from the strategy. The Expression stage had previously always been a potential stumbling block in the development of the self-help strategy because of the danger of people becoming overwhelmed by feeling.

> We should feel sorrow, but not sink under its oppression.
>
> Confucius, 551–479 BC

So, breathe a large sigh of relief if you have been anxious about this stage. However, don't take yourself off your guard completely. I must warn you that if you are not very used to expressing feelings, you may experience a few initial difficulties with your emotional control. This is because you may not yet know how to stay in the driving seat of your expression or have not yet had enough practice in doing so. If we are not in full control, emotion can rapidly well up without us realizing it is doing so. You could then become fearful of expressing any further feeling. Commonly, people say that they are afraid their tears will never stop or their frustration may escalate into dangerous rage.

Another reason why you may decide to push down on your emotional pedal is that if your feelings are overly intense you could become exhausted. Expressing deep emotion depletes our energy reserves. I have often seen this happen when people are very aware of needing to be able to return quite quickly to crucial tasks such as working, looking after children or simply cooking.

Finally, if you are a novice at expressing feelings, you will need to take extra care if the hurt from which you are healing has been a major one. The same advice applies if the hurt is similar to one that you have experienced before and may not yet have fully healed. You will remember we looked at these phenomena in Exploration.

But don't be overly alarmed by these warnings. (And don't go into denial!) Help is at hand. Here are some tips which will help you to stay in control while you are working through the Expression stage.

TIPS TO HELP KEEP YOUR EXPRESSION UNDER YOUR CONTROL

Tip 1: Watch Out for Your Early Emotional Signals

The first and most important trick is to know and watch out for the very first signs that a feeling response has been triggered. These are the physical sensations that will tell you that an emotional response has been physiologically ignited. Let me describe a couple of my own as examples.

When sadness is beginning to well up inside me, I now notice a tingling in my nose. This happens well before I would even notice any sensation in the tear ducts behind my eyes. When I am beginning to feel annoyed, I now notice a sensation of tightness around my forehead. This happens well before I start to tap my fingers or my feet.

Obviously, your nose may never tingle and your forehead may never tighten. This is because these early sensations vary from person to person. I know someone whose early signal of tears is clenching their hands, while for another it is closing their eyes. Different early warning signals for anger can include tightening of shoulder, leg or stomach muscles. When you are trying to discover what yours may be, it is a good idea to keep particular watch on the weak points in your body. These are the areas that tend to be first affected by the extra stress of negative emotions. It is no coincidence that I suffer from sinus problems and that the two early warning signals I described earlier are located in the sinus area. Someone who has a skin disorder may notice theirs as a slight itch or a change in skin temperature. Another person with a troublesome digestive system may notice theirs in their stomach.

The chances are that you won't discover your very earliest signals for a while. But the more often you use this strategy to heal minor hurts, the easier it will become. This is because with minor hurts we are relatively more relaxed and therefore have more awareness of what is going on in our bodies.

Tip 2: Learn and Practise Quick-Fix Calming Techniques

Calming down your emotions is very different from repressing them. Basically what you are doing is switching off your primitive 'Jungle Speedway' auto-responses. Once you have done this you can then take more conscious control. You are able to deal with your feelings in the way you would have done if they had been processed along the more sophisticated 'Wisdom Way'. This allows you to decide when and how to deal with them.

There are very many methods now available in books and on CDs but sometimes it is easier to learn the basic techniques with a relaxation teacher. The trick is to keep experimenting until you find the technique that works for you. The three that I am going to describe below are my own favourites and have also worked for the majority of my clients.

Magic Mental Reviver

Lie down or sit down cross-legged in a Lotus-style position.

- Close your eyes. Consciously relax any tension in your body. Check that your face, jaw, hands, arms, legs and feet are loose. Allow yourself to sink into and/or feel supported by whatever surface you are sitting or lying on.

- While mentally following the passage of your breath as it goes in and out, take three or four slow deep breaths. Sometimes it helps to imagine your breath as one colour as it is drawn in and another as it is expelled.

- Now let yourself breathe naturally and easily, while slowly counting backwards from 50 or repeating the alphabet like this: ab ... bc ... cd ... de ... ef ... etc. Each time a thought enters your mind return to counting from 50 again or the start of the alphabet.

- Finish by allowing your mind just to gently float for a few minutes. (Your body should feel light and 'floaty' as well.)

- Repeat, if you have time.

Positive Affirmation Meditation

- Relax your body using the technique above.

- With your eyes closed, say a very short appropriate affirmation sentence as you breathe in and out (e.g. while breathing in, say, 'I am'; as you breathe out, say, ... 'confident ... in control ... courageous ... capable', etc.).

- As thoughts, worries or ruminations come into your mind, gently return the focus to your chosen affirmation for one to five minutes.

Scenic Symbol Meditation

- Relax your body as before.

- Close your eyes and focus your mind's eye on a chosen symbol or scene which conjures up an image of success or a feeling of peace and relaxation (e.g. a handshake, a goal being scored, a sunset on the beach or the face of someone you admire immensely).

- Use your imagination to examine your scenic symbol in minute detail. Try to recall the impression it made on each of your senses.

- Be aware of the positive feeling that has been recreated within your body. Every time a thought comes into your head, refocus your mind's eye on the symbol again.

An Imaginary Stroll

- Close your eyes and relax your body with a few deep breaths. Release any stored tension from stressed muscles by slowly tensing and releasing them.

- In your mind's eye, imagine that you are taking a five-minute slow circular walk around a beautiful and peaceful place such as a garden, a mountain, river or seaside. You could choose an indoor location if you prefer such as a house, church or museum that also has calming memories for you. As you walk, take care to notice as much detail as you can and appreciate the colours and forms and scents that are appealing to you.

- Before opening your eyes, choose a place to sit down for a minute and focus your attention on one favourite thing while focusing on your breath as you gently inhale and exhale.

Tip 3: Appoint an Emotional Security Guard

An 'Emotional Security Guard' is my title for someone who is at your side during this Expression stage. Their role is to ensure that you do not do yourself or anyone else any harm while you are expressing your feelings. Such people need to be selected with care. In an ideal world, they would possess all the following characteristics. In the real world, you would be using this list as a guideline and be aiming to find someone as near to this model of perfection as you can.

Emotional Security Guards

Ideal Characteristics

The kind of person who would be an ideal choice to accompany you through the Expression stage would:

- Be currently emotionally stable and not under duress;

- Have the ability to remain cool and calm when deep feelings are being expressed;

- Have no emotional agenda themselves in connection with the hurt you are working on (e.g. they don't or didn't love, like or hate key figures in your 'story');

- Have the physical strength, or ready access to someone who has, to be able to restrain you if this should prove necessary;

- Be assertive enough to tell you if you are wavering from the task (e.g. intellectualizing or even joking about the hurt or your difficulty in expressing);

- Have enough self-confidence to admit their limitations and ask for help should this be necessary.

The person you choose to help you during this stage may also be useful in the next one – Comfort. In the following chapter I will be giving you similar guidelines for choosing an ideal comforter. You will see that some of their credentials are the same. If you find someone who ticks all the boxes for both tasks, lock them up and throw away the key! They are too valuable to lose. I could instantly start a very long queue for the use of their services.

Speaking seriously on this subject, there are plenty of people around who can perform both tasks to a good-enough standard. But they may not realize that they can, so they may not offer their help. You may have to ask them. When you do, it is important to tell them clearly what you need and don't need from them.

If you are reluctant to ask for their help because you are afraid that they could find it difficult to say No, make it easy for them. Give them an opt-out and an assurance that you can cope without them. Here are some different scripts to give you an idea of how you could do this:

- *'I am currently trying to emotionally heal from being ... I am now looking for someone to just sit with me while I explore and express some of my sadness. I realize you may be too busy, and if so I would really understand and would be happy to ask someone else.'*

- *'You know I was recently ... Well I am really making an effort to get over this and move on. I've reached a stage where I know that I need to feel and let go of some of the emotions that I have been trying to avoid. I know that this may be difficult for you as it may remind you of ... but I do so admire the way you have coped and I would appreciate it so much if you could be with me while I try to do this. If you think it might be too hard for you or you are too busy, please say No. I promise you that I'll understand and will find someone else.'*

- *'I think you already know that when I was ten I ... This trauma is still creating problems for me today. So I am working through a strategy which I believe will help me heal from the emotional scars and finally put it behind me. One step involves trying to get in contact*

with the emotions I felt at the time but have never been
able to express. I don't want to get really angry or
break down, I just need to feel a little of the emotion I
have repressed in order to move on. As I admire the
way you are always so calm and cool in times of crisis, I
would love you to be there for me one afternoon while I
take this difficult step. But I don't know what kind of
pressures you currently have, so do feel free to say No
and I will ask someone else.'

Then you can test them out. Although this might not seem a 'nice' thing to do, it is important for the progress of your healing to have the right kind of support. They may not even realize that they have started going down an unhelpful track. For example, they may start trying to get you to see what happened in a positive light (i.e. jumping you forward to Perspective). Or they could become emotionally involved themselves and be urging you to forgive or forget which might be their default philosophy even though they don't live by it in normal circumstances. Such responses are common when people witness someone in distress as a result of a hurt. They are understandable but not helpful. So have the courage to say so.

Tip 4: Be Fit

If we are in a state of physical weakness we do not have so much control over our emotions. Perhaps you can remember not being able to stop yourself from starting to cry when some minor upset occurred during a time when you had lost some sleep. Similarly, if you have a heavy cold or a headache, aren't you more likely to lose your cool if someone is rude to you?

So try to plan your Expression sessions at a time when you are not likely to be over-tired. If you are feeling ill, postpone them.

It is also a good idea to eat something before you start and have some food and water at the ready if you are having a long session. Hunger and thirst can affect our emotional control as well.

Tip 5: Get Cleaning

Get mad, and then get over it.

Colin Powell

This may sound a frivolous suggestion amongst all the other more serious ones but I am including it because it is the one that works best of all for me. Upsetting phone calls are truly good news for my kitchen! I find that cleaning and tidying are the quickest way for me to get control of my feelings. So this is what I tend to do if I want to stop crying, trembling or even shouting. I think it works because it distracts me with a positive challenge and releases my physical tension at the same time. I felt much less silly about including this technique here when I heard a story on the radio about a banker who was kidnapped and kept in a hole ten feet beneath the ground for four months. He said that when he reached complete despair, he used housekeeping to help himself. He would clear every strand of straw off the floor and proudly recalled that he got rid of 28 slugs in one day.

So try leaving your house in a dishevelled and mucky state before you start your Expression session!

If you are not into cleaning, I am told that gardening or some form of DIY does the trick for other people. Again, experiment until you find what works best for you.

HOW LONG WILL IT TAKE TO COMPLETE THE EXPRESSION STAGE?

This is a question I am often asked. Who would relish the idea of hurtful feelings being around for a long time? Of course, I cannot give a definitive answer. So much depends on the degree of hurt and the personality and circumstances of each individual. But what I can say is that people are often surprised at how quickly it can be completed.

For everyday small hurts you may only need a few minutes of quiet time, especially if you have the space and time to express your feelings soon after the experience. But old hurts and the more troublesome ones will usually need at least one or two sessions of a couple of hours. For these, as I have already suggested, it is a good idea to plan special sessions into your diary. (Otherwise they may never happen as everyone wants to put them off!) One client of mine who had a backlog of hurts to express from her childhood and two broken relationships, decided to set aside one day a month for four months as 'Heal and Feel' days. This worked brilliantly for her and, as it happened, she only needed to use three of these special days. The last one she used for giving herself some comfort, which took her neatly on to the next healing stage, Comfort. This person, however, was self-employed and it was relatively easy for her to set her own working agenda. You may need to programme your healing work into a busy schedule organized by others. If so, you must allow adequate emotional 'warm-up' and 'cooling-down' time. This is why you need to plan sessions of two or more hours.

Most hurts are adequately dealt with in one session, but some may take a few more. It is important to go at a pace that is manageable with your lifestyle and give yourself as long as you need. You will know when you have done enough by the way your body feels. You should be able to sense a release of tension. People often let out a deep sigh and start to breathe more evenly. The emotion may not have left you, however. You may still sense, for example, your sadness for a loss or your disappointment at a big setback. Your healing is not, after all, over. You have several stages to go yet.

SUGGESTIONS FOR ENCOURAGING EMOTIONAL EXPRESSION

Whatever your needs in relation to Expression may be, there are even more ways to ensure that you make the very best use of your time. These following suggestions will save time and often have an added benefit as well. Because they can make the whole experience of Expression more pleasant, we are less likely to procrastinate and find something less painful to do.

If you have a major hurt to heal, it would probably be wise first to practise Expression on minor hurts using the above suggestions. You will then be less worried about losing control and you will be able to do this step much more effectively.

Use Exercise to Release Some of Your Stored-Up Tension

If you have been holding on to a hurt for a long time, you will undoubtedly have stored up a good deal of tension in your muscles. It will help to release some of this before starting Expression by doing some form of gentle physical exercise. Beware that if you exercise too strenuously, you could increase your tension. The following exercises would be good ones to choose, but there are others as well:

- Swimming

- Stretching

- Yoga

- Pilates

- Walking

- Dancing

You may need to try a few out unless you know which suits you best. Be aware of where your tension is most often stored and work on those muscles in particular.

Select and Prepare a Room That Will be Conducive

First and foremost, find a place where you can be private and where you are not likely to be disturbed. Unless you have an unusually large working environment or house, this will mean choosing a time when no one else is around. Ensure that all phones are off and if it is necessary, put a note on the door to stop people knocking.

If you are at home or have a private office, you can make the room even more conducive by pulling down the blinds or closing the curtains. Low lighting helps because it relaxes us and therefore makes our feelings more accessible.

As you don't want to leave your space until you are finished, provide yourself with some drinking water and tissues. If you think you can be overheard, a cushion can also be useful just in case you need to muffle any loud sound. After reading the rest of these suggestions you may want to use some props to help you Express. If you think you might, make sure these are easily accessible as well.

Go to the Scene of Your Hurt

Sometimes people choose to do this stage in a special location away from their home. For example, it can sometimes be helpful to return to the place where your hurt took place. One woman booked into a guest house in the town where she was brought up, because her hurt dated back to her childhood. A man I know drove to the car park of the firm that made him redundant. Another went to sit in a quiet corner of the pub where he and his ex-fiancée had spent many happy times. Several others have chosen to go to a graveside or cemetery when their hurt had been the loss of someone dear to them.

Should you choose to go to a public location as these people did, you must be confident that you can handle the feelings that may come up. Make sure that you have a 'bolt-hole' at hand. This could be a quiet car park or even a bathroom where you could go afterwards if you need some privacy to let go of any tears or tension. You could of course also take an Emotional Security Guard with you or at least have one ready for service at the end of a phone line.

Use Creative Visualization to Recreate the Scenario

An alternative to returning to a real location that could re-kindle your hurt is to use your imagination as you could have done in Exploration. This can be done in a specially prepared room as described above or a secluded location. When I lived in Yorkshire, I used to go on to the moors near my house to express frustration and anger. Now, when I am at my house in Spain, I can use a nearby beach which is often deserted. If I am in a town, I will often use a quiet corner of a church or a beautiful park to mentally recall the trauma or the person whom I have lost, and gently release some feelings of sadness or disappointment.

Treat Yourself to Time in a Specifically Designed Centre

If you have the money and the time, an alternative place to do some Expression work might be a centre which offers the space to be quietly reflective. More and more of these are springing up now and you don't usually have to belong to the host group to use them. Most are accustomed to people using their facilities for emotional healing and will allow you to do so discreetly and in peace. A search on the internet will bring up a wide range of alternatives.

Similarly, some yoga, meditation and massage centres can offer suitable facilities and would give you other benefits as well. These kinds of treatments and activities can help facilitate the release of tension and therefore help bring emotion to the surface. Sometimes they also have staff on hand whose services could be used to give you a professional Emotional Security Guard.

Last but not least (of course!), you could join me on one of my Reflect and Recharge weekend breaks on the south-west coast of Spain, which are ideal for doing work on Expression.

Use Music to Conjure up the Right Mood

Play music that evokes for you the emotion that you want to Express. You could even record your own compilation. My husband, who has a much greater knowledge of music than me, often makes a special compilation for me to use in my groups. I explain the kind of emotions that I am likely to be working with, and he finds the music that will evoke them. But I always have calming music to hand as well to use when necessary. I suggest you do this too.

> . . . previously unfelt or forgotten emotions begin flowing through me, released by the trigger of the music.
>
> Jason Webster: *Duende*

Recreate the Scent

Our receptors for smell are directly connected to the limbic system, the most ancient and primitive part of the brain, which is thought to be the seat of emotion. So scents are an extremely fast way to evoke feelings. If you can recall what smells and scents were around at the time of your hurt, recreating them may be very useful. These could be, for example, a perfume, a food, grass or smoke. Sometimes you can achieve the required effect by just recalling the scent in your imagination.

Watch an Emotionally Relevant Film or TV Programme

This is another emotional 'warm-up' technique that I have used with great success in workshops. It can be time consuming, but well worth it if it works for you.

Read

A quicker and perhaps easier technique is to dip into a book of relevant quotations, poetry or a moving autobiographical account of a similar experience. When my daughter Laura died, I knew just the book that would help me, so I ordered a copy straight away. It was Isabel Allende's *Paula*. This includes an account of her daughter's death and her own experience of grief. Because I knew that this book would evoke very deep feelings in me I did not open it until I knew that I would have the time and space to deal with them. (But interestingly, having the book waiting in the wings beside me was wonderful. I knew that it would play an important part in my healing – and it did.)

Write

After Laura's death I tested out for myself another very powerful way to conjure up feelings. It was a technique that I had suggested many times to clients to good effect. It involves simply writing to the person you lost in a book that is destined to be read by you alone. I wrote every night for many months – this generated an opportunity to Express some of my feelings in a private and safe way.

Many people use journal writing as a method of Expressing. The broadcaster John Diamond did this when he knew that he was dying of a brain tumour. Much of his journal writing was shared with the general public through his internet blogging, his articles for newspapers and the extracts he recorded for the radio. By doing this he was also attracting a good deal of healing Comfort (our next stage) as many thousands of people were moved by his sharing and sent their good wishes.

Finally, I'd like to pass on some wise advice which the UK's Children's Poet Laureate Michael Rosen sent me. He wrote some wonderful poetry after his son's death which helped both him and many other adults and children trying to heal from a loss.

'You have to be utterly honest with your feelings. If you try to deceive yourself – or if you write something that you know yourself is untrue – it will come back and bite you. The part of yourself that knows that what you've thought or written is untrue will constantly nag at you and make your sadness worse. It'll do this by confirming the apparent fact that you are worthless. "Not only did you let that person die, but you also lie about it. How low can you get, eh?" If on the other hand you are honest, in an almost ruthless way, it seems to have another kind of effect altogether. If it's something you write, you can take a pleasure in the fact that at least you're seeing things clearly, that at least you've found words and phrases and cadences that capture the sadness and wretchedness. And there is, as the poet said, a terrible beauty in that.'

Use Art

You can use art in two ways to help you Express. Either you can create your own work (by, for example, painting, creating a sculpture or making a photo collage) or you can use other people's. I was lucky enough to meet a young sculptor just after Laura died. He was so moved by her story and meeting my other daughter and myself that he offered to make a bust of her. We have this beautiful work of art in the memorial garden that we created in our home in Spain and a copy of it in our sitting room in England. It has proved to be an invaluable aid to helping me to release feelings (as well as giving immense Comfort). I am not sure quite why the sculptures work so much better for these purposes than photos of real-life scenes do, but I have heard other people say the same about portraits of loved ones and paintings symbolizing disasters and wars.

Enact a Drama

One powerful way of evoking feelings is to use a chair or cushion or symbolic object to represent the perpetrator or perpetrators of your hurt or the object or people you have lost. You can then start talking to them. When using this method, honesty is vitally important. So either do it on your own or with someone with whom you can be completely yourself. If you have not used this technique before, always start by having someone with you because it can generate deep emotions very quickly.

Another even more powerful option would be to attend a Dramatherapy or Psychodrama group if you are lucky enough to have one of these in your locality. These have the advantage that you will be working with people who are likely to truly empathize with your feelings and will be there to give you high-quality Comfort when you need it.

Share on the Internet

I have already mentioned this method in the last chapter and given some warnings. Although the internet can be useful to kick-start a healing process by the time you have reached this stage, I think that it would be less risky and more satisfying to obtain face-to-face support. But if the internet is the only option for you, try to find sites where you can see people's faces and have live interaction. Feelings are often Expressed more honestly and movingly through body language rather than through words.

However, some internet geniuses are working on the limitations of internet communication in relation to emotions. One company has come up with an ingenious method of sharing feelings through colour. Have a look at this link to a Mood-Sharing programme which could be a useful way to record as well as Express your feelings: http://www.cmu.edu/news/archive/2007/February/feb6moodjam.shtml

EXPRESSION IN A NUTSHELL

To experience the bodily sensations of the feelings which were triggered by the hurt and allow them to be Expressed bearing in mind that:

- You only need to feel some rather than all of the feeling.

- Repressed feeling can well up suddenly and uncontrollably, so select a safe secluded environment.

- You may need an Emotional Security Guard to watch over you.

- You need well-practised emotional control techniques.

3. Comfort

Your aim during this stage is to find a way to be emotionally soothed by some kind of caring attention. If your hurt has been very minor, this attention could be self-administered. But for the vast majority of emotional wounds, it is best given by someone else. The most luxurious and most effective dose of Comfort is a cocktail of high-quality consoling care from both yourself and someone who truly loves you, combined with a generous dash of empathic support from a range of other people.

Sounds inviting? Perhaps, but I doubt it. I say this because this is the step that has proved to be the biggest healing stumbling block for most of my clients. Frowns and quizzical looks are the common responses when I begin to talk about Comfort to them.

In contrast, Comfort is the stage that people with high emotional resilience find the easiest. When I talk about it to these lucky people, they smile. They have no problem coming up with examples of how they can and do give it to themselves and they have no shortage of people in their lives who can and do administer it to them on a regular basis.

So it seems that this stage is likely to be the most crucial one of all. That's tough news when you fear that it may be the most difficult one for you, however pleasant it may appear to others. The better news is that we have ways of making the medicine easier to swallow!

First, you need to examine what may be underlying your difficulty. This will help you to become more motivated to try it out. Secondly, you can apply some specifically targeted curative action.

COMMON DIFFICULTIES WITH COMFORT AND HOW TO OVERCOME THEM

Below are some examples of responses which I typically hear from people who find the very thought of this stage daunting. It is very possible that some will ring bells with you. If so, I hope my comments and suggestions will be helpful.

I suggest that you read each one through rather than just scanning the headings for the most familiar. This way you could encounter some other helpful information about Comfort and gain a better understanding of other people's difficulty with it.

Remember that the more sensitively applied the Comfort we give to others, the more we are likely to receive in our hours of need.

'It would feel self-indulgent so it wouldn't work.'

Comfort is not self-indulgent; it is self-nurturing. The difference between these two styles of behaviour is enormous. The first is decadent and selfish and arguably unnecessary. The second is an essential natural survivor response to hurt. It is an important part of healing. Comfort can be, and often is given mutually between people when they share the same or similar hurt. It is not therefore intrinsically selfish. You might not have been aware of this difference. Usually the reason for this kind of misunderstanding can be traced back to the negative or confused messages about self-nurturing that you picked up in childhood from the parenting you received, your religion or other formative influences. Was this the case for you? If so, do this little exercise:

Action

List the differences in personality, needs and values between yourself and people whose ideas about giving and receiving Comfort might still be holding you back.

'Comfort has not felt healing for me in the past.'

There are two main causes for your kind of problem. First, Comfort might have been given too soon. Comfort is something that most people feel immediately compelled to give to others when there is a hurt. Unfortunately, the strength of the urge can be so great that it is often given too early and then it is not effective. Unless you have been through the Exploration and Expression stages, even if it is given sincerely and well, you won't be emotionally open to receiving it. You might even push it away.

Some time ago, I was watching the England football team do just this after a very major disappointment in the World Cup. At the end of the game, many people flooded on to the pitch to give them a consoling hug. Some were actually pushed away. The hugs that were given were received by figures of stone. The stunned players obviously did not want them. This was a poignant example of Comfort being given far too soon. In relation to their emotional healing needs, what was probably even worse for the players was the reaction of the rest of the country. Cries of disappointment were quickly replaced by endless analytical talk about why the game was lost and how it would go down in history. In other words, the country by and large leapt straight from an all-too-brief period of Expression into Perspective. It was a dramatic example of how uncomfortable this stage of healing is for English people. In contrast, in other countries, people can be openly sobbing into each others' arms for hours on end after a very disappointing sporting defeat.

A second reason why Comfort might not have worked for you before is that the type you received was defective. Perhaps it wasn't authentic. This happens frequently even though the person who is giving it is trying their best to be sincere. Even our nearest and dearest often find it difficult to understand why we are feeling hurt or upset about something. They could have a different personality make-up or may have been trained to react quite differently in similar circumstances. I recently watched two families deal very differently with a big disappointment.

Both the Brown family and the James family had equally bright nine-year-old boys. Both had applied for the same local school which was renowned as being by far the best in their area. Both were rejected.

The Brown family told almost everyone in earshot about the bad news and their disappointment was plain to see on their faces. In doing this they both Explored and Expressed their hurt. As a result, they and their son received Comfort from colleagues, friends and their extended family in a spontaneous and natural way. It came obviously in the form of consoling hugs from some close friends and family.

But it was also given verbally by very many friends, neighbours and colleagues in the form of simple and sincere expressions of sympathy and empathy such as:

'Oh how awful'; 'You must be so disappointed'; 'This system is so unfair'; 'There shouldn't be such a big difference between schools'; 'I know how disappointed my daughter was when she didn't get in.'

My guess is that neither the Brown family nor the people making these comments were even aware that they were contributing to this crucial stage of emotional healing. But it was highly effective nonetheless. Buoyed up by this support, the family have now decided to appeal the decision. As yet, we don't know whether this appeal will be successful, but I am convinced that even if it isn't, the hurt caused by this disappointment will have been healed.

The James family reacted differently. Mr James (supported by nods from his wife) was reported to have said to his crying son:

'That's life – in this country nowadays. Too many people; too few resources. The government should stop the flood of immigrants. But they never will. So best to forget it and just make the best of it. Neither your grandfather nor me had a good education and we got by. Don't show them you care. I'll get us tickets for the match on Saturday – what do you think?'

Although Mr James' love for his son is not in doubt, his handling of the disappointment was not healing for anyone but, most especially, not for his son. At nine years old he is unlikely to be able to put his feelings behind him as his dad suggested. I would guess that, like so many other children who have had this kind of cold comfort from a parent, he might have secretly cried under the bedclothes that night. If he did, he would have probably been castigating himself for being 'silly'. He would therefore have caused himself even more emotional pain and put a severe dent into his self-esteem.

So, in a sincere effort to comfort his son (and probably himself), Mr James in fact seriously sabotaged the healing of the disappointment. By offering to buy tickets for the match he was confusing Comfort with Compensation (our next step). But worse still, he hadn't even allowed Exploration and Expression to do their preparatory work so that any Comfort that might be offered by others would have fallen on stony ground.

Although I can't be sure, I would hazard a good guess that Mr James habitually responds to emotional hurts in this way, so his son is likely to act similarly when he reaches adulthood.

Action

Finish this chapter! By the end you should have a good idea about what is good-quality Comfort, who is best able to give it to you and when it should be sought and given. Then reflect on whether the Comfort you have experienced previously was truly the kind that would have healed you.

'I am always seen as strong and the comforter of others.'

This confession usually has to be teased out of people, but it is extremely common nonetheless amongst my clients. This is particularly true of people from the helping, teaching and policing professions and women who have spent a great deal of their lives looking after children and/or ageing relatives. They are usually excellent at giving Comfort to others, but find it so difficult to ask for it for themselves. This is because they have to keep a kind of wall around their own feelings much of the time and it feels scary and strange to let their guard down to show their hurt and their needs.

Sometimes this 'acting strong' behaviour has become a habit that needs gently challenging with some reality testing. When they tentatively try asking for and taking Comfort, they find that the world doesn't crash down around them.

But some cannot do this because they believe too deeply that by showing their weakness and asking for Comfort, they run the risk of either losing their jobs or losing the trust and respect of the people whom they help. There is little foundation for this belief though I must admit that I have seen it turn out to be correct on a fair number of occasions. There is indeed a minority of people who cannot cope with seeing their 'helpers' and role models of strength in a state of distress. This means that they will turn their backs, however guilty they may feel about doing so. I have worked with a number of clients whose guilt about doing this to their parents was still playing havoc with their self-esteem and family relationships long after their fortieth birthdays. Most had been teenagers at the time when their parents' marriages broke down. I have also worked with several doctors and a police-, man whose careers were all unfairly negatively affected because they requested Comfort from colleagues.

So, if this is your problem there may be a few grains of truth to back your fears. But should these be allowed to deprive you of the healing Comfort you need and deserve yourself?

Action

Motivate yourself first by writing down what you risk losing if you do not allow yourself to accept Comfort. Then make a Contingency Plan to deal with your fears about the consequences of letting down your emotional guard. Depending on your situation, this could range from just scripting out an assertive, self-protective response to someone who you think might query or laugh at your request for Comfort, through to making enquiries about alternative jobs if you seriously think your career is at risk. It should also include making a note of the names of alternative people you could turn to for Comfort should your request be refused.

'I don't know anyone who could or would comfort me.'

This may be because you are in the category above. But it could also be that you live or work in an apparently Comfortless environment. Many zones in our large cities are now like this. Factors such as the following are largely responsible:

- Long stressful working hours that leave people with little energy to care for 'number one';

- Housing and town planning that discourages neighbourliness;

- Multi-culturalism that leaves people confused about what is the right and wrong way to show concern and offer help to people from different backgrounds.

If this is true for you, remember that underneath all these factors, the human heartstrings are as strong and serviceable as they are anywhere else. They may simply need a bit more tugging to get them into action. Those of us living in an apparently low-comfort zone such as London know this only too well when the city has a crisis such as the bombings on our transport network. It was heartening to see that when fellow citizens really needed Comfort, there was absolutely no shortage of it to be had from fellow strangers. Many deep lasting friendships were also formed as a result of the mutual caring, sympathy and practical help that emerged so quickly and spontaneously.

Action

Put photocopies of pictures of people giving Comfort to each other on a wall or fridge where you will see them regularly. This will remind you that the heartstrings are there.

Then, demonstrate through loud and clear Expression that you need Comfort or assertively ask for it in the following way:

- Prepare what you are going to say first, so you can edit your request to the minimum number of words you need (stressed people respond more readily to messages which are short and to the point).

- Make it easy for the person you are asking to give you Comfort by telling them directly what you would like them to do (e.g. give me a hug/make me a cup of tea/ just sit with me for ten minutes while I cry this out of my system).

- Rehearse your request so you can say it confidently and without any off-putting whiny tone creeping in (See page 108 for a guide on how to do this assertively).

'I would be too embarrassed to ask.'

Sounds silly? Yes, it does to most people. This includes the people who say it. They often prefix the statement with 'I know it sounds silly but . . .'

But once again a pre-programmed belief or emotional blueprint response is the cause – not the person themselves.

Action

Hopefully the work that you did on your auto-responses in Expression might help (see page 64). Re-read it. Because Expression and Comfort are so linked, it should give you a clue as to where and why you might have picked up that old message lodged in your head: 'You should be ashamed of yourself for needing Comfort.' Then think about the people you have Comforted in the past and ask yourself if they should have been ashamed to need this kind of help. Your answer will almost certainly be No, and this old message should no longer be troublesome.

'I couldn't cope if I was refused.'

This is essentially a self-esteem problem. It is not to do with coping, it is to do with feelings. People with high enough self-esteem can take this kind of refusal in their stride. They know that there are many reasons why people might refuse and that there is always a slight risk that this could happen. So they prepare themselves.

Action

Give yourself a self-esteem boost. If you still don't know how, just dip into my *Self-Esteem Bible* and follow one or two of the 365 tips.

Then read on and take special notice of my guidelines for the Ideal Comforter on page 105. Approaching the right kind of person will significantly reduce the risk of this happening.

'I am a very private person.'

This may be. But lurking underneath this statement is often a touch of arrogance. If it had words it might say: 'I am clever and more resilient than most other people – I don't need to depend on anyone else for support. I wouldn't entrust my hurt to anyone.'

Alternatively, it could also point to a self-esteem problem. You may not yet have learned to truly love and respect yourself in spite of your weaknesses.

Action

Deal with any arrogance by looking at how some people you admire greatly lean on others for support. I had to struggle myself with this problem and I used Nelson Mandela's example to help me. Like me, he is an introvert, but publicly acknowledges his need for Comfort from others.

Deal with any self-esteem issues as above until you have more confidence in yourself, and make sure you take your Comfort in private.

'I don't like physical contact, especially when I am upset.'

Fine, if that's how you *really* want it. Comfort can be given very adequately without any physical contact at all as you will see from my suggestions later. But, people who make this statement often secretly wish they were able to take a hug and enjoy it. If this is the case for you, there are two main possible causes of your problem which you should consider looking at.

First, your natural inclination for giving and taking physical Comfort may simply have not been encouraged and developed. It could be that you were born into a non-cuddly family or national or religious culture where Comfort is largely expressed in non-physical ways. If this is the case, physical Comfort would not feel repellent but just a bit strange because it is not 'normal' behaviour for you. When we are distressed, a sense of familiarity helps us to feel safe and secure. As you know, I was brought up largely in old-fashioned children's homes where positive physical Comfort was almost never available. Although I have now learned to feel more comfortable with hugs, I still have a tendency to hide in a quiet corner if I am very distressed.

Secondly, for a very much smaller minority of people the cause of the problem could be more serious. They may have suffered a psychologically damaging experience from physical contact. For example, those who have been physically assaulted or abused in childhood by someone they should have been able to trust almost always find physical Comfort difficult to take. This is because when we are distressed we often feel like a child so the fear/back-off response is likely to be automatically ignited.

One little girl who I knew personally, at around four years old, started to forcibly push away any attempts to give her physical Comfort when she was upset. Before that time, she was the cuddliest child you could imagine and continued to be so whenever she was happy. You can imagine how frustrating this was for her mother and anyone else who wanted to cuddle or hug her when she so obviously needed that kind of comforting.

Six years later, while examining this little girl for another problem, a paediatrician discovered that she had been, and was probably still being, sexually abused. After intensive investigation, it was decided that the most likely perpetrator was her natural father, so all access to him was stopped and the family moved to a new area so that she could start life afresh. Gradually, she became very much more physically relaxed with her family and her girlfriends. However, when in her teen years she started to have relationships with boyfriends, the problem re-emerged. When talking to her mother after one quarrel with a boyfriend, she started to confide in her about it. She could not understand why she would suddenly 'go cold' on people she loved. She recalled doing it as a child and feeling bad because she knew how hurt her mother was. Fortunately, she agreed to start having some psychotherapy.

Because this girl's problem was rooted in early childhood and was the result of a major abuse, she needed professional help. If you think your problem has been caused by having your trust in intimate physical contact damaged, I would suggest that you, too, seek some professional therapeutic help if you want to overcome it. Alternatively, you could try a good self-help organization where you will meet people who have had the same experiences. And, if you need Comfort in the meantime, don't forget, there are other ways to obtain it as you will see in my list of suggestions towards the end of this chapter. Non-physical Comfort is not 'second best', it is just different. All that matters is what works for you and enables you to move on emotionally.

If, however, you think the root of your problem is more to do with not having had the chance to develop the habit of taking physical Comfort, then try these suggestions.

Action

Start experimenting with minor physical contact from people who are close to you, such as allowing someone to give you Comfort by touching your arm or holding your hand. Then, when this begins to feel normal and easy, you could experiment with accepting an arm around your shoulder. You may need to explain to some people that you prefer not to have a big enveloping hug for the moment. You can soften your refusal by making the physical contact you can take yourself. You could, for example, take their hand and give it a squeeze while saying thanks. When you feel ready, you can start asking for what you need yourself. 'Could you just hold me for a moment? I'm feeling a bit shaky,' is a lot easier to say than you might think right now, because you are taking the initiative and feel in control.

In the meantime, look at the suggestions below for gaining Comfort by other means. If that is, after all, the only kind with which you can feel at ease, don't think you cannot be healed.

'There are people who are much needier than me.'

Yes, there are, and there always will be. Your problem is partly due to insufficient self-esteem and partly due to an irrational belief that there is a finite supply of Comfort to go around. Let's address the latter as we have already dealt with self-esteem issues.

One cause could be rooted in your early experiences. Perhaps when you were growing up you were at the back end of the pecking order in terms of Comfort. This often happens in families – even when the parents think they are bending over backwards to be fair. Some children (particularly the extrovert kind) are better at grabbing their parents' energy and attention; some (for example those with problems) are more needy because they are continually hurting; some (particularly the introverts) get little attention; and some of course become favourites.

Another cause could be that your parents (or others from whom you tried to get Comfort) constantly made you aware of people who were worse off than yourself. You may have had a surfeit of this kind of talk:

'Think yourself lucky, it didn't leave you blind, legless or homeless.'
'John didn't always come running to me the moment he was hurt ... and hasn't he got more to cope with than you?'
'Remember those children we saw on the TV in that Iraq orphanage last night? Now they were brave and smiling in spite of everything.'
'Okay so you didn't come top this time. Just think of those who have never been clever enough to be top at anything.'

Sometimes these kinds of messages aren't delivered quite so directly. They may be picked up rightly or wrongly from an interpretation of action or circumstances. For example, I had a client whose parents were doctors in a missionary centre in Africa. She couldn't recall them ever saying anything like this and she was sure they wouldn't do this. But we did conclude that she had developed this belief about being less deserving of Comfort than most from just observing her parents' selfless devotion to their work with grossly underprivileged families. She also remembered them not being available (because they were doing important work) to Comfort her when she encountered minor hurts such as unfair and unkind comments from local children about her colour and comparatively privileged lifestyle.

Recalling this client's story has reignited an uncomfortable one of my own. When my daughter Laura was fifteen, I can vividly recall her screaming abuse at me on this very subject. She told me that I didn't really care about her problems. I didn't think they were as important as those of my clients. As you will no doubt have gathered I was a working mother. Because of my own childhood and understanding of child psychology through my professional training, I made a very special effort to make my children feel that they, and their needs, would always have priority in my life. But my children knew about the kind of work that I did which, at that stage of my career, was almost exclusively with a mental health charity.

Her words shocked me first into defensive argument and then later into guilt and self-reflection. As a result we talked (i.e. Explored). I accepted that perhaps I had allowed the balance to tilt in favour of my work a little too often recently. She Expressed her feelings of resentment and I Comforted her. We agreed a Compensation weekend away together at a horse-riding centre (and I hate riding!) and then talked generally about the pros and cons of working mums (Perspective). I think our jointly administered 'treatment' worked because I never heard any of those types of comments again and know she had every intention of becoming a working mother herself.

I have shared this story to illustrate how this sabotaging belief about Comfort can be picked up even if you are not living in the shadow of saints. Perhaps if the daughter of the missionary doctors had had enough confidence (or cheek!) to confront her parents, this belief would not have taken hold in her subconscious mind. She might then have felt much less guilty about taking the Comfort she deserved for her hurts.

Action

If you believe that the cause of your problem is the first kind I suggested, then some simple re-programming of your belief system should be sufficient.

Compose three countering statements similar to my examples below and use them to affirm the human right that you have been denying.

- I have as much right as any other human being to be comforted.

- I have a right to heal from any emotional wound.

- The more emotionally resilient I am, the better able I will be to help others in need.

Write these affirmations out on an attractive card to carry around with you. If you are a computer wizard, create a screen saver with the same message. Read the affirmations out loud twice a day for a month.

If you think the cause of your problem may be due to residual emotional hurt from the past, you can start the healing process right now by Exploring and Expressing with a good friend who is understanding, but doesn't share your sabotaging belief. After that force-feed yourself a generous dose of Comfort!

'I'm a man; it's different for you women.'

Perhaps, but we may not be as intrinsically different as you think. Things are changing for men in relation to Comfort. When I did some research 20 years ago in the UK on how men heal from hurt, I found that there were big differences between men and women. Women needed to interact with people to obtain their Comfort. Comfort was obtained through empathic words and hugs of sympathy. After an emotional hurt, men tended to throw themselves into problem-solving or some other kind of action. Achievement was their preferred route to Comfort. They said it made them not only forget, but feel more secure. (Interestingly, achievement may be a subconscious route to getting the physical Comfort they may want. It does after all stimulate human contact in the form of warm handshakes, pats on the back, arms around shoulders and even hugs.)

A more recent research project carried out in the USA has shown that although men did give a bit more advice more often than women, and women are slightly more likely to provide support by affirming their friendship or offering help, there is only a slight difference in the way they administered, gave and took support.

Maybe the differences in these two studies are partly to do with differences in national culture, but my experience and observation confirms that there is a growing trend for men to seek and give Comfort much more openly.

Now I have hopefully demolished any arguments you may have had against Comfort, let's turn our attention to how you can ensure you will receive it.

RECEIVING COMFORT

Comfort can come in all sorts of shapes and forms and from all sorts of people. It can sometimes be given by people you don't even know. I have received many empathic letters from readers who heard about my own trials and tribulations. Similarly, I have had many healing facial signs of sympathy, warm handshakes and hugs from strangers who have attended my talks and heard my stories. After Laura's death the priest from the town where we have a house in Spain offered to hold a mass for her. This was a great honour as we are not Catholics and do not attend the church. After the service, there is a custom there that all the members of the congregation go up to the bereaved to give their condolences. I can still recall the warmth of that healing Comfort I received through having hundreds of hugs from people I had never met before.

Sometimes Comfort can be given and received by simple moments of stationary silence. We do this formally to honour the memory of public figures who have died and it gives Comfort for those who grieve. On a smaller, more intimate scale, we can be Comforted by someone just being stunned into speechlessness and passivity as they empathize with our feelings. Nelson Mandela, in his autobiography *Long Walk to Freedom*, talks very movingly about how comforted he was by a friend who simply held his hand without saying a word after he received the news of his son's sudden death in a motorcycle accident.

But wonderful and welcome as these kinds of Comfort are, there are even more healing kinds. These tend to come from certain kinds of people who happen to be able to give Comfort to you at this particular time and for your particular hurt. Here is a list of the main traits that an ideal Comforter may exhibit.

PORTRAIT OF THE IDEAL COMFORTER

An ideal Comforter is a person who:

- Genuinely cares about you and your welfare;

- Is able clearly to communicate their sympathy and empathy. At best, you might expect them to do this with words and/or deeds. At the very least, they would be able to communicate through their body language that they are sincerely upset that you have been hurt;

- Is able to get fairly accurately 'in tune' with how you are feeling. Even if they have not had the same experience, or have, but reacted differently, they are able to say convincingly, 'I know how it must feel to have lost someone precious/been let down/to have been unfairly deprived/to have been blamed unjustly,' etc;

- Can accept your feelings for what they are. You wouldn't hear them saying, for example, 'You shouldn't feel sad, you should be glad to see the back of them; you shouldn't be angry, they were just doing their job.'

- Can be non-judgemental with you. Even if they inwardly think you made a mistake or were largely to blame, they should be able to hold on to their 'I told you so' and 'You are your own worst enemy' opinions when giving Comfort. (But remember that they could also be useful later when you reach the Perspective stage.)

- Is able to maintain emotional control. They would be able to feel along with you, but also have the ability to stop themselves crying their guts out or thrashing around in a rage when they see you Expressing your pain and distress;

- Is able to listen without needing to share their experiences and advice while giving you Comfort. (Again, they can do this at a later stage.)

- Respects the level of bodily Comfort that you want. So they wouldn't insist on hugging you if that's not what you need – even if they may feel the urge to do that themselves and think that it would help;

- Is assertive enough for you to feel that they will say 'no' when they cannot or do not want to help you;

- Would be willing to support you as you move on through the next phases of healing;

- Is the kind of person whom you would be happy to give Comfort to if ever they needed it;

- Would not expect their kindness to be considered as a debt that needs repaying;

- Is able to take full responsibility for the repercussions that helping you might bring to their own life. So you might hear them say, 'Don't worry about the time, I can make it up later/Don't concern yourself with him, I can handle his moods/Ring me anytime, I am quite capable of surviving without the odd night's sleep.'

- Has currently enough physical and emotional energy to be able to give you the kind of Comfort you need;

- Is capable of and willing to take action to protect you if you should need this kind of help while you are in a vulnerable state. (Ideally, this would be done with your permission. But very occasionally emotionally hurt people can be so upset that they are not capable of knowing that they may need protection from themselves or others.)

Obviously the above list is a challenge for even the best Comforters to live up to all the time. So remember to use it as a guide and that good-enough people are often easier to be with than perfect saints. The following exercise will help you to judge whether or not you may be better off getting your Comfort from several people rather than one person.

Instant Exercise

● Think of someone you know from whom you might consider taking Comfort. Use the Portrait of the Ideal Comforter to check out whether they have enough of the characteristics listed to be able to help you. (Very few people are able to fit this bill fully.)

● Use this list to check out some other people who may also be able to give you Comfort. You should be able to see that you can have most of these characteristics met by having your Comfort from several people rather than just through one person.

HOW TO ASK FOR COMFORT

As we have already discussed, many people are too busy, stressed or simply shy to offer Comfort spontaneously. But if they are asked in an assertive way that gives them plenty of permission to say No, they will often be delighted to oblige. Here are some examples to guide you.

● Darren, a relatively newly qualified barrister, had lost an important case. He had talked it all through with colleagues and Expressed his feelings with his wife, but chose to ring John, an old friend, for some Comfort.

John, you know that case that I told you about several months ago? We lost it finally. In a way it's a relief that all those months of stress are over, but at heart I feel gutted. I thought together we had put a good case. I wonder if you would mind sharing a pint with me some time to talk it through. I've been sounding off to Jane at home and that's helped a lot. She's been great.

*But having a night out with you is just what I think
I need right now. But, it is not urgent, I'm over the
worst, so it can wait if you're busy.'*

- Angie had been having some personal development
  sessions with a counsellor. They had been looking at
  some events in her childhood that had brought up a
  good deal of buried hurt. She rang her friend, Babs,
  as she needed some extra comfort.

*'Babs, you know I have been having these sessions. Well,
I have been getting really upset about that time when
my mum and dad split up. I am doing well with the
counsellor but I'd just like to spend some time with you.
I just know you'd understand how I am feeling. I'm
basically okay but just need a little bit of support right
now. Could we have lunch some time? Please do say if
you'd rather not. I know you have a lot on, with coping
with Jamie right now. I can easily ring someone else
and we can always meet up later on.'*

- Des had just received an affidavit from his wife's
  lawyer. He thought he was okay emotionally about
  the divorce, but seeing this legal document had
  made his blood boil up again. He had talked it
  through with his own lawyer who was excellent, and
  he had let off some steam by playing a few games of
  squash.

  Now he felt he needed just to get away from
  London for a few days and get some peace and quiet.
  He had an aunt and uncle in the rural county of
  Dorset whom he really liked, and who were always
  inviting him down, so he rang them.

*'Hi, Uncle Bill. I know this is a bit of a blast from the
past. How are you both? Well, I've not been too good to
be honest. I expect you've heard from Mum and Dad
that Gill and I have split up. I was in a pretty bad way*

*at first and didn't want to see anyone. I'm basically
okay now, but have just been dealing with the affidavit.
It's shaken me up a bit and I thought I'd like to take
up your offer of a break down by the sea. Is there any
chance I could come down one weekend next month?
I don't want to talk about it all, I just need to have
some peace and quiet and I know you'd give that to
me. I fancied shaking the dust off my fishing gear so
I hoped we might be able to have some time out in the
harbour. I'd really enjoy that. But do say if now's not
the right time. I could always go up to the Lakes for a
weekend. But if you are free it would be just great to be
with you and Auntie Irene for a few days.'*

RECEIVING IMPERFECT COMFORT GRACEFULLY FROM OTHERS

This is a lesson I have had to learn, and it is also one that I have
had to teach to very many people. Unfortunately, those who are
in need of Comfort are not the only people who have hang-ups
with it; many of the givers do too! This means that however
sensitive and kind they may be, they may suppress their compassionate urges or may misfire, irritate or offend when they do
attempt to give Comfort. You may have already experienced this
and it could well have surprised you. It often isn't until we are
hurt and in need of Comfort that these problems and hang-ups
become evident.

Giving Comfort is actually an innate response. We humans are
programmed to react automatically with compassion whenever
we sense someone is emotionally hurt. Tears in particular trigger
this response. But then so do other body language signals as well,
such as a bowed head held with hands, or desperate-sounding
screams. But this ability to empathize can cause problems. Many
people today are not very comfortable with their own tears or
anger. This means they may go into emotional shut-down mode,

and appear unmoved or even uncaring. Also, because they have switched off their emotional antennae, they no longer have the tools to sense what is needed and pick up on the non-verbal messages which should indicate that they are getting their Comfort-giving wrong.

Others may be needy because your experience has triggered off a painful memory for them, so that they cannot stop themselves from telling you their sad story. You may find this Comforting at first but, because it is really the last thing you need at this stage, you will soon get so irritated that your feelings might well show. At a later stage in your healing, sharing with such people can be very useful for both parties, but it can be highly counter-productive right now. I have heard and personally received many tales of apology from poor Comforters well after the event. A client recently told me a moving story of meeting up with his father after years of separation. The son had distanced himself from his family after they had reacted with a very uncomforting response to him failing his degree. As they talked it became clear that his father had cared deeply about his son's disappointment, but had just been out of his emotional depth in the situation.

Similarly, last year I received a lovely email from one of Laura's school friends. She apologized profusely for just sending a card and not having been to the funeral over ten years previously. She said Laura had always been so special and inspirational to her that she couldn't accept that she had died and couldn't then deal with the grief. Her email gave me some bonus Comfort which I will never tire of receiving. It also added to my empathy for the 'inadequate' Comforters amongst us and prompted me to write this section. But enough of the sympathy and understanding for now; how do you deal with these common problems when you are hurt and needy yourself?

First, try not to be offended if someone doesn't get the Comfort right for you. People often comment that this is the time when you hear people say, 'It showed me who my true friends were.' I am sure this disappointment with friends (and relatives) in times of stress is caused by the kinds of problems I have just highlighted.

This does not mean that you have a responsibility to solve these problems for them – even if they are your nearest and dearest. All you need to do is to receive whatever they *are* able to give gracefully. You may not need ten cakes or want a stiff bearhug, but you can focus on the spirit behind the gauche actions and grating words and express sincere gratitude. But that's that. Don't do what so many do and spend so much time and energy with these people that there is none left for acquiring the kind of quality Comfort you really need.

You must be assertive and say when enough is enough. I know this can seem very hard to do, but remember it is not impossible! The best approach is a well-rehearsed direct statement or request such as:

> *'I am so grateful to you for ringing/visiting. But I now want to be very quiet/need some time on my own/must talk to a few other people, so I'd like to say goodbye for the moment.'*

The second-best approach is a white lie. This is actually much riskier, even though it is often regarded as a cop-out from taking the direct approach. But it can nevertheless be justified, especially when faced with exceptionally thick-skinned or emotionally disturbed 'wannabe' Comforters. If you are going to use it, take care to make sure that your story is simple, so you won't trip up on it and those around you will support your fictitious excuse.

SUGGESTIONS FOR GIVING COMFORT TO YOURSELF

I find frequently that hurt people 'go blank' on me when I ask for examples of self-nurturing and treats which they could use for Comfort. So here are some simple suggestions. These will ensure that you have no excuse for opting out for want of ideas, time or a good deal of money! But, bear in mind that the best kinds of ideas for your self-comfort are going to be your own.

- Prepare yourself a favourite meal. The classic 'mother's cooking' or 'nursery' type often works best rather than complicated dishes.

- Give yourself a delicious refreshing drink. Go preferably for the nutritious or non-toxic kind. You are still emotionally unstable so you need to watch out when drinking any alcohol. This kind of drink is also dehydrating and you may well have lost fluid during the emotionally charged Expression stage.

- Have a long luxury soak in a hot aromatic bath.

- Indulge yourself by giving yourself an unusually extended time to read a novel or magazine or listen to your favourite music.

- Take yourself to an exhibition or gallery or park where you know you will find uplifting beauty that you never usually get enough of.

- Buy tickets for a show, concert or sports game that you would not have otherwise attended.

- Buy yourself a present, but ensure that it is one you can afford so that you are not worrying about your extravagance.

- Pick or buy yourself a bouquet of flowers.

- Go on an excursion to a place where you will feel at peace.

- Treat yourself to a short stay at a quiet guest house or hotel.

COMFORT IN A NUTSHELL

The purpose of Comfort is to allow yourself to be soothed by the caring attention of another person or yourself, bearing in mind that:

- You may first need to resolve your hang-ups about taking this kind of help.

- You must choose your Comforter carefully.

- You must make assertive and sensitive requests and prepare for a possible refusal.

- Imperfectly given Comfort can be healing if it is given generously and received gracefully.

- Self-administered Comfort doesn't have to eat away at your bank balance, but it does need quality time.

4. Compensation

During this Compensation stage our task is to ensure that we receive some form of satisfying amends for the hurt we have suffered. These can vary widely because each emotional hurt merits its own appropriate type of Compensation. This is because if it is going to work from an emotional healing point of view, the amends must be relevant to:

- The degree of pain and damage that was caused;
- The kind of emotion that the hurt triggered;
- Any deficit that may have resulted;
- Our priorities and preferences.

Later I will be giving you many examples of Compensation in action ranging from small treats for a minor disappointment to long-term projects designed to make amends for serious child-hood deprivations or traumas. But ultimately you will be responsible for judging what kind of Compensation would work for you.

However appealing this stage may sound, I am well aware that it might not seem right now to be a priority. If you have completed our first three healing stages, you should be feeling a good deal more positive and energetic. You might prefer to put the 'angst' behind you and get on with your life. It is possible that you have a pile of tasks on your back-burner because everyday jobs often become side-lined when we are hurt. But try to remember that although your big healing drama may be over, your wound is still fragile. It may no longer be giving you pain, but it is unlikely to have much resilience. Another emotional knock could easily re-open it. And because you are still emotionally vulnerable, you are likely to be more prone than usual to making unwise choices or mistakes. Rebecca's story below illustrates this danger.

Rebecca's Story

Rebecca was in her early thirties with a young son and pre-teen daughter when she discovered that her husband had developed a gambling habit. Little by little, she uncovered a mountain of debts that her husband had secretly accrued. The consequences to the family were devastating. The house had to be sold and the children taken from the private schools that they had just settled down in. The marriage also became unsustainable as Rebecca had completely lost trust in her husband. She experienced little difficulty with the first three stages of her emotional healing. She had plenty of friends who supported her through these and also helped her with the practicalities of starting life as an impoverished single parent. But, mistakenly, they thought that after six months on her own, Rebecca was ready to hit the dating scene and find a rich new partner! So they clubbed together and bought her membership to an expensive Lunch Introduction Service.

Their generosity worked. Within a month Rebecca was in another relationship. A few months later she and her children were living with this man and his daughter, a widower in his extensive house. Everyone was blissfully happy at first, but within a year the relationship had broken down and Rebecca had sunk into a state of despair. Luckily, a class teacher spotted a change in the behaviour of Rebecca's daughter Amy, including frequent missed days at school. After talking to Rebecca it became clear that she was depressed and had little energy or will to fight battles with Amy over the minor ailments she claimed made her too ill to go to school.

The teacher suggested that Rebecca, rather than Amy, needed the help and advised her to seek counselling. During her sessions with me she accepted that she had not fully healed from the hurt of her husband's deceit and its effects before launching herself into the dating scene. She believed that this had caused her to feel overly grateful to her new partner for 'rescuing' her from her financial hardship and single-parent status. This imbalance of power in the relationship caused her to give in continually whenever there was an argument over ground rules and decisions about her children's care and discipline. She had now started to do the same with her daughter Amy.

Rebecca's hasty leap from the Comfort stage of healing into a new relationship is not uncommon. Perhaps you have seen it for yourself.

Alternatively, you may have seen another kind of common mistake at this stage of healing. Once they begin to recover their strength and sense of personal power, many people start turning their attention to securing negative types of Compensation.

NEGATIVE COMPENSATION

There are two main types that we need to look at: Just Punishment and Revenge.

Just Punishment

The pursuit of an eye for an eye and a tooth for a tooth may be the kind of satisfaction you currently feel justifiably motivated to seek, but is it even remotely possible? For example:

- A hefty fine rarely feels like an adequate punishment for a heartless thief who has robbed someone not just of sentimental treasures, but also of their sense of personal security.

- A prison sentence for a violent attacker or a drunk driver is hardly adequate compensation to those who are left physically or emotionally disabled by their actions.

- Pay-outs from companies who engage in heartless 'restructuring' are never enough for their redundant workers.

- Generous divorce settlements frequently feel like inadequate compensation for the loss of a home, family and trust in others.

- The sacking of a teacher who has bullied or abused a child into a state of paralysing fear can never satisfy an angry parent.

- A lifetime of self-castigation won't heal the hurtful regret that you would feel if your selfishness has destroyed a relationship with someone you truly loved and respected.

Perhaps these are extreme examples, but I hope they make the point that the kind of punishment that is possible (and others may judge as fair) may not seem to be so in the eyes of those who have been emotionally hurt.

Even when just punishment does seem to be a realistic possibility, securing it can be highly costly in terms of energy and finances. And it is not a task that can be done efficiently if you are functioning below par. At this stage of your emotional healing, it is unlikely that you would have recovered your normal energy and brain functioning capacities. If you are going to pursue that line of action, it is better to do so after completing your emotional healing.

If instant action has to be taken (for example, to catch a criminal or protect others), try to delegate this task to others until you are healed. Call on the services of a professional agency or someone who has had a similar experience. The latter should be emotionally healed themselves, but still have the memory of the hurt and so can be fired up by empathy and the promise of vicarious satisfaction from seeing justice done. If delegation isn't possible, you may have to take action yourself. If so, don't kid yourself that you won't need emotional healing after you have secured justice. Make sure that you also have the kind of positive compensation that will meet your psychological needs.

Revenge

When we are emotionally hurt, it is very understandable to feel a passionate thirst for revenge. A quick search on the internet reveals that this need also generates good business. There is a growing number of companies who are now ready and willing to help emotionally hurt people indulge this primitive response. For a price, you can arrange for:

- Dead flowers to be sent to an ex who has jilted you or had an affair;

- Annoying anonymous spam mail to be sent to your bullying boss;

- Prawns to be sewn into the curtains of a company whose customer service 'stinks' (perhaps they have been rude and uncaring);

- Fake parking tickets for a friend who has let you down.

These businesses seduce with the promise of pleasure and satisfaction. But, in my opinion, they are falsely trading on the 'Revenge is sweet' assumption. Perhaps they can provide you with an instant buzz of satisfaction. But this kind of feel-good factor is not only short lived, it also often leaves a bitter aftertaste.

Revenge is in essence a 'fight' survival response. At one stage in human history, before society had laws and the means to enforce them, it may have been in our interests to exact it. Nowadays it seems to me to be an overly risky and usually unproductive game for hurt people to play. We may fool ourselves that it will 'teach them a lesson', but the reality is that it rarely does. It is a highly ineffective method of changing personality or behaviour. The cruel will laugh it off or give back harder than they got. The ashamed are already deterred. Their own uncomfortable conscience has done the trick.

Another reason why revenge doesn't work as compensation is that it dents our self-esteem. Only a psychologically disturbed sadist can feel self-respect after intentionally hurting or embarrassing another person, even if revenge seems justly deserved. Most reasonable people regret taking revenge later. They end up feeling ashamed or guilty, especially if their revenge has been 'over-the-top' as it often is, if it is taken before emotional healing is fully completed. If we want to move on positively and effectively, we must guard rather than deplete our self-esteem.

But if after hearing all these negatives about revenge you still have a burning thirst for it, here is some good news! A great deal of satisfaction and some healing can be derived from indulging in *fantasy* revenge. You should now have enough emotional control to let your imagination safely run a little wild with some pay-back fun.

How can fantasy revenge be satisfying? The principle is very simple. It works in the same way that positive visualizations work. Because our emotional systems cannot make any distinction between an event that is happening inside our heads and one that is taking place in the real world, it produces the same physiological reactions for both. So we experience the same feelings of pleasurable satisfaction with imagined revenge as we would with the real thing . . . but without the risks.

Revenge fantasies may not appeal or be necessary for everyone. But they do seem to help some people (myself included!) move on, so here are some tips if you want to give it a go.

Tips for a Preparatory Indulgence into Fantasy Revenge

- Don't hold back on your fantasy. The more wildly absurd and unrealistic your mental images are, the more satisfaction you may feel. For example, one of mine was to imagine a very large flag flying over Leeds Town Hall declaring the 'sins' of a certain person to a shocked fast-gathering crowd below (. . . and yes, they are going to remain nameless in this book!).

- Try drawing or painting images of your fantasy revenge. Then get into action such as splashing paint over the picture or ripping it up and ceremoniously burning it.

- Write a short story about the person or thing getting their 'come-uppance'. Then play it in your head as a mental movie. Finish with a happy-ending image of you. I am sure that fairy stories and film series such as Superman and James Bond owe much of their long-lasting popularity to their revenge fantasy endings.

- Invite a good friend to join in and add to your fantasy exercises. This can be fun and give you some extra Comfort at the same time. It can also act as a safety precaution. A good friend will stop you from overdosing on revenge and can direct you back into the more important healing work you now need to do. A good parent takes this role when a child's natural revenge fantasy play starts to destroy an expensive toy or hurt a younger sibling.

Once you have finished your fantasy exercise, hopefully you'll be more motivated to find a truly healing form of recompense for yourself. So let's look now at how you might be able to do this.

COMPENSATION IN ACTION

Nowadays Compensation is most often thought of in relation to securing financial recompense from the person who is guilty of having hurt you. In fact, the frequency with which people tend to knee-jerk into this kind of action has given rise to the term 'Compensation Culture'. But although securing financial compensation can be emotionally healing, it is certainly not the most common kind that we use for emotional healing purposes. And even when it is secured, its main contribution would be to fund the acquisition of other more emotionally satisfying means of recompense.

But even when financial recompense is a possibility, you may find that it is not a route that you *want* to take. An experience I had is a very good example of this phenomenon.

As a result of a mistake made during immediate after-care following an operation, I became seriously ill and needed a further six surgical procedures over the next few months. This extended trauma affected me emotionally as well as physically. I was away from home in an area where I had no friends. I was unable to work and had to cancel many plans including a long-awaited work trip to Moscow and writing this book. Due to my weak state and the drugs I was on, I couldn't even think clearly and found it hard to make even the smallest decisions. Much of the time I was dependent on others to do everyday tasks. As a result, I started to feel powerless and useless. At one point I became so low that my family were more concerned about my emotional health than my physical recovery which was progressing relatively well.

Interestingly, almost everyone who heard this story reacted

by talking about the financial compensation I could and should claim. But even though the whole experience had cost me a very considerable amount of money, at no point during or since the experience did I think I wanted to seek this kind of recompense. (One of the reasons was that I knew the staff that were treating me had taken responsibility for their mistake, and were bending over backwards to put it right. You will see that this aspect of my story is especially relevant to Step Seven: Forgiveness.)

However, after examining my behaviour later, I can see that once I had healed to the Comfort stage (that is, I was no longer tearful and had enjoyed much TLC), I automatically started to give myself the kind of recompense I really wanted. Before thrusting myself back into my work, I sensed that I needed a lift to my spirits and something practical to do that also involved me looking forward positively. So I gave myself the permission and the time to divert my energies into finding the new homes in Spain and in England that before this trauma we had decided we wanted. In spite of many frustrating hiccups that often accompany house moves, this project worked wonders in terms of my emotional healing. The exciting challenge and change lifted me out of my depression and helped me to move on to achieve a sense of Perspective concerning this experience.

This particular Compensation project worked because it was addressing the aspects of trauma that were most hurtful for me. The strategy propelled me into a state of powerlessness and pessimism. That was particularly scary and distressing for me as it echoed the state I had been in 40 years previously when I had attempted suicide.

Many friends looking on thought I was quite mad to engage in such a difficult project straight after my ordeal. But I was certain that I was on the right track for me, even though I was not consciously thinking of what I was doing as being Compensation. Because I am so practised now at this game of emotional healing, once again my auto-pilot had chosen and administered the perfect remedy.

Until you become as well practised, you will probably need to give some conscious thought to planning the best kind of Compensation to match your hurt and your needs. When helping people to do this, I have found it can be helpful to think in terms of making up for a deficit that the hurt has left you with. The areas of deficit that people can be left with vary enormously as you will see in my examples below. When there has been a major hurt there may be quite a few areas in need of replenishment. To help kick-start you into thinking what might work for you, here are some examples of Compensation that I have seen working well for others.

A Deficit of Self-Confidence

1. Jim failed a professional accountancy exam which he was expected to pass easily.

   - He had a weekend break and took a book on study skills with him.

   - He asked his boss for some mentoring, and the relationship between them improved considerably.

   - The result was that he was given more responsibility and job satisfaction even before he had passed the exam.

2. Julie was deserted by her husband who fell for a woman 20 years younger.

   - She used part of the settlement for a make-over at an exotic spa.

   - She attended my 'Moving On' course in Spain and decided to return to live in the countryside where she had always felt more 'at home'.

3. Chris was accused of being 'stand-offish' at work.

    - She bought herself a bangle that she had previously resisted buying because it was an 'unnecessary extravagance'.

    - She took a communications skills course and her relationship with her children improved – as well as those with her colleagues.

A Deficit of Optimism

1. Raphael had suffered a series of disappointing sales figures.

    - He changed his holiday plans. Instead of going abroad, he spent an enjoyable time chilling out at home. This included taking his son to races at Silverstone, which he had always promised to do, but had never had the time, and reading some inspirational books by business gurus.

    - He made networking a priority. He booked two conferences and entered Business Link meetings into his diary for the next year. He also booked on a course to improve his networking skills.

2. During a visit to Israel, Marsha found herself near the scene of a suicide bombing.

    - She took an adult education course in Peace Studies and met many inspirational people who became close friends.

    - She began training as a lawyer with a view to specializing in Human Rights.

A Deficit of Financial Security

1. Katy had her purse containing her holiday cash stolen
    at the airport.

    - After helping her to report the upsetting theft to
      the police and her insurers, her friends said they
      would club together to give her some money to
      buy a new purse. She resisted her inclination to
      decline their offer and used part of the money
      to buy a new colourful purse in a sale.

    - She herself added some money to the sum that
      was left over and treated herself to the matching
      handbag as well.

2. Darren was unexpectedly made redundant.

    - He used the spare time to clear out and revamp his
      house. He held a car boot sale and with the
      proceeds had a series of consultations with a career
      advisor specializing in business start-ups.

    - He gave himself a month's 'sabbatical' in order to
      think. He took himself for a low-cost back-packing
      break in Vietnam. (He said that this was his best
      ever holiday and more exciting than his usual
      five-star spa holidays.)

    - He started a highly successful small eco-cleaning
      business with the redundancy pay-out.

A Deficit of Social Support and Friendship

1. Gael (yes, me!) had to move house to an area where she had no friends.

    - She started a book group and tango club and made many friends.

    - She started a newsletter and social events for the local community and made many more highly interesting and supportive friends.

2. Barbara had a major fall-out with her best friend.

    - She reconnected with several old friends through a friendship website.

    - She joined yoga and French classes and made new friends.

A Deficit of Trust in Other People

1. Pierre's relationship with his girlfriend ended when he learned that she had not been honest about her past.

    - He arranged to spend some extra enjoyable time with a select number of friends whom he trusted implicitly and who had never deceived him.

    - He joined a high-class dating/friendship agency where people are strictly vetted and found new friends and a soul-mate.

2. Gael (me again!) was conned by a number of salespeople on a holiday trip.

- She went on a market shopping spree with a truly street-wise friend. She asked her friend to handle her negotiations and acquired some great compensatory bargains.

A Deficit of Trust in Mutual Dependency

1. After his managing business partner misappropriated joint funds, Rob took his share of the business capital and:

- Gained an MBA;

- Set up in business on his own.

2. Lesley was prematurely widowed.

- She asked her sister to care for her children while she came on one of my 'Revitalize your Career' courses to reassess her options in the current world of work.

- She started training as a teacher, which gave her quality time with her children during school holidays, but was also more suited to her strengths. She specifically chose a university with an excellent nursery, family accommodation and a ready-made social life.

A Deficit of Opportunity to Use Your Full Potential

1. Jose had to leave school prematurely to work as his father died and the family needed his financial support.

- He did an Open University degree while continuing to work in a car factory.

- He asked for a sabbatical to do a Masters in engineering which was granted and paid for by his company. In addition, they promised him promotion on his return.

2. Giles Long (an inspirational friend of mine) developed a serious cancer in his teens that required the amputation of most of one arm. At the time he was destined to become a champion swimmer.

- He took up intensive training to adapt his swimming style and won three Paralympic gold medals and was awarded an OBE. He now uses his experiences to motivate and inspire people in the business world to take up challenges and deal with setbacks.

A Deficit of Energy and Inclination for Fun

1. Nicole had breast cancer and had to have a long series of breast reconstruction operations.

- She bought a new wardrobe of clothes and had a new hairstyle.

- She took up dancing.

2. Adele was brought up in social isolation as her family lived in a war-torn country and her father had to go into hiding.

- She joined a musical drama group to help develop her spontaneity and meet fun people.

- She went on a series of singles holidays which included many social activities.

3. Isabel had an exhausting five years of looking after her mother while holding down a stressful job. She reluctantly agreed to take her mum to a home for Alzheimer's sufferers.

    - She turned her house into a 'spa' for a weekend. She filled the fridge with nutritious and delicious ready-prepared food, locked the doors and turned off her phones. She spent the weekend in a dressing gown reading romantic novels while soaking in scented baths.

    - She treated herself to a series of personal training sessions with an easy-on-the-eye coach!

I hope after reading this wide variety of examples you have a good idea of what positive Compensation is all about. You may even have started to take similar action yourself because, as I have already said, each of these steps should follow on quite naturally one after the other. You may also have found that Compensation has started to happen without you having to even think about it, because it has been a by-product of your new situation.

It certainly is healing to count the unexpected blessings that emotional hurts sometimes bring, but remember these may not be enough for you. They may not address enough, or any, of the kinds of deficits that we have looked at.

Finally, there is one more kind of Compensation that I want to introduce. It is gaining some healing for yourself by making recompense on behalf of someone else. This is often used when a loved one has died prematurely. A relative or friend may find that they can gain vicarious Compensation for themselves by achieving things that their lost loved one might well have liked to do themselves. I heard one of the parents of a victim of the *Marchioness* boat disaster on the River Thames say in an interview that they were motivated to pursue the ten-year battle for compensation for the victims by focusing on the way in which this victory would go towards making up for the things their daughter would no longer be able to achieve in her own life.

Similarly, my daughter recently ran the London Marathon to raise money for the school we are building in Uganda in memory of my other daughter Laura. She said that she was motivated by thinking that her sister would have loved Africa and would have wanted to do something to help there.

Instant Exercise: Analysing the Deficits After an Emotional Hurt

Reread the list of examples to prompt you into thinking about what deficits you may have and what you could do for Compensation. If you cannot think of anything that you could do, ask a friend to help you come up with some ideas. Most people are only too willing to do something constructive and positive to help. They may need to read this chapter first so they have an understanding of what might or might not help. But remember, *you* must feel that what they suggest is relevant to your hurt and needs. It won't work otherwise.

At this stage of your healing, remember that you only need to achieve good-enough Compensation. You can always do more later on. My daughter ran her marathon eleven years after her sister's death, and as you will have noticed from my other examples, some Compensation plans need years to reach their objectives. You will know when you have given yourself enough for now when you begin to feel a sense of distance from your hurt. This will be an indication that you are sliding naturally on into the next stage, Perspective.

COMPENSATION IN A NUTSHELL

The purpose of Compensation is to ensure that you have some recompense for the deficit that has been caused by your hurt, bearing in mind that:

- It must be relevant to the hurt and the feelings that were triggered by it.

- It is not about seeking revenge or just punishment, even if the perpetrator deserves either.

- Financial compensation alone is never good enough Compensation for emotional hurt.

- It can be short term or long term, and even be necessary for the rest of your life.

5. Perspective

A pessimist sees the difficulty in every opportunity; and the optimist sees the opportunity in every difficulty.

Winston Churchill

We have arrived at our last essential step. Our aim in completing this one is to gain a better understanding of how and why the hurt occurred. By doing this, we not only often gain new and different perspectives on the hurt; we also acquire some learning from the experience which may be helpful to us when we move on. We feel more forewarned and forearmed to face any other hurt that we may meet en route.

As a result of engaging in Perspective we also, more often than not, identify some other positive benefits that have arisen as a result of having and dealing with the hurt. This is how we find any opportunities there may be to turn the 'crisis' into an opportunity. The process of this stage is similar to preparing a 'White Paper' or an 'Independent Enquiry' after a disaster has happened. These are often done quite some time after the event and can take a good deal of time to complete. The people who are appointed to take charge of this important work have to be emotionally distant enough from the hurt to be able to undertake a meticulously balanced investigation and come to an objectively analysed appraisal and conclusion. Their aim is to do this so thoroughly that a line can be drawn under the event and those concerned are able finally to move on.

Even if your hurt seems to have been caused by factors that make no sense and cannot be blamed on any specific person or thing, you will always find something to be gained from working through Perspective. I have not known one single hurt that has been unable to give some wisdom or have some other positive benefit.

In this healing stage, it is as though you must appoint yourself to head up just this kind of enquiry into your hurt. Some of you might have already started to get into Perspective before you even opened this book! This stage must be the most popular healing 'job' in today's world. Indeed it is so enticing to modern man and woman that it is common for people to leap straight into it the moment a hurt is felt by us or anyone else. This is particularly true (but by no means exclusively) for those whose personal strengths are an excellent match for the job that you need to do.

For example, a long-time friend betrayed a deep trust I had thought we shared between us for their personal benefit. In the evening of the day I heard this news, my daughter telephoned me. She caught me in a distraught state. In her efforts to help me regain the calm that she knew I had to have, she told me that I needed to remember that this hurt, however difficult to bear, was only another relatively minor 'blip' in the story of my life's set-backs. She reminded me of how happy and successful I generally am and how many good friends I still have who haven't let me down.

In other words, my daughter was trying to help me to see my hurt in the wider context of my life's experience. (Doing this is one of the main tasks we have to undertake in this stage of healing. As we will discuss later, we use our intellect to help us take the Big Picture view of our hurt. This helps us realistically to assess its significance.)

At the time of our telephone call, I was nowhere near the Perspective stage of healing. I was still reeling from shock and in too much emotional turmoil to even start Exploring what had happened. My daughter (unlike me) is inclined by her nature to respond to problems in an analytical and pragmatic way. These innate character strengths of hers have been invaluable to us as a family and helped guide us through many crises. On hearing my distress, my daughter spontaneously did what she does best. She fast-forwarded straight into Perspective. (As it happens, because I understood what she was doing, it didn't matter. Indeed I could be, and was, moved and comforted by her words. Also, she had started to give me the kind of help I was more ready and willing to take at that time.)

> Every experience, however bitter, has its lesson, and to focus one's attention on the lesson helps one overcome the bitterness.
>
> Edward Howard Griggs

But my daughter was not the only person to try to rush me prematurely into Perspective. Several friends with very different personalities and dominant strengths did the same. Many started theorizing about what might have caused my friend to do what they did. They wondered about their personality and extenuating personal circumstances. One wondered if I had been overly trusting and reminded me of other times when this tendency of mine had led to trouble; others blamed outside influences and external economic factors.

These friends were also doing an important Perspective task. They were focussing on the cause of the hurt to see who or what was responsible for causing it. But again I was not ready for this kind of task. Luckily I was able to spot what was happening and told my friends that I was trying very hard to hold back on examining possible causes because I was still in such an emotionally upset state. Again, I was really fortunate because they all switched tack and gave me great support to do what I needed to do first. This was (as I hope you have already guessed), to Explore what happened by talking it through in detail and then Expressing my feelings while my family and friends patiently and empathically listened or gave me Comfort.

Has my story rung some bells for you? I wouldn't be at all surprised if it had. Even if it is not programmed into our genetic make-up to fast-forward to Perspective, most of us will do so more often than is good for our healing. Understanding why people may do this helps to make us more tolerant of ourselves and others when we leap prematurely to Perspective. So let's briefly look at three of the main reasons why we tend to do this in the 21st century.

First, our modern education systems nurture and exercise the analytical thinking centres of our brains. Rationalizing and intellectualizing are habits that are continually reinforced because these generally provide the most efficient and successful ways to meet our contemporary basic needs and deal with problems. So turning to Perspective immediately after a hurt tends to feel sensible and 'normal'.

Secondly, because our world today is so fast-paced and competitive, we almost always want to get to the goal-posts as fast as we possibly can. At some instinctive level, perhaps we also know that Perspective is at the end of the essential healing journey so we are understandably keen to rush ourselves and others there.

Thirdly, self-help gurus (like me!) have made too much impact. We have bred nations of amateur psychologists who habitually talk and theorize about why people behave in the way they do. We gurus have also successfully passed on into common knowledge many of the key tricks of the trade for transforming black moods into positive ones; the main 'tricks' being variations on positive and rational thinking techniques which also happen to be the key tools we use to achieve Perspective. It doesn't help that this knowledge is now also prevalent in the workplace. In spite of the efforts of the Emotional Intelligence movement, there is little tolerance for weeping and wailing in today's world of work. It is almost always preferable to quickly administer a dose of some simple psychological tricks and then move people straight on into Perspective.

So be understanding if someone does this, but make sure that you stand your ground. Most people who take this fast track are, like my daughter and some of my friends, doing so in good faith. They do not have the knowledge that I am privileged to have about healing hurt. Because I know what Perspective looks and sounds like when it is in action, I can spot its presence. This means that I can be on the look-out for it and take action when it is

intruding prematurely into my healing. Trust that you will achieve
much better Perspective when you are fully ready for this stage.
The kind that you achieve without having worked through the
previous healing stages is like a cheap plaster bandage. Its benefits
are destined to be short-lived. The pus will soon begin to seep
through and the wound can be easily re-opened by the slightest
pressure from a new emotional knock.

It is from the 'downs' that I learned – it was such a rich
experience.

Isabel Allende, on the death of her daughter

Let's now assume that you are ready to make the most of this
very satisfying stage and examine what needs to be done. I have
already referred to a couple of the tasks it involves, but its job
description does include a few more. In summary, there are five
main areas which you need to check out:

1. *Context*
    We examine events leading up to the hurt and the
    surrounding circumstances in which it occurred.

2. *Patterns*
    We look for any familiar sequences of feeling
    responses and behaviour to identify whether there is
    evidence of a negative habit.

3. *Responsibility*
    We look at what caused the hurt and we decide,
    when appropriate, who or what was to blame for the
    hurt and the reaction it triggered.

4. *Significance*
    We decide how meaningful this hurt is in the Big
    Picture view of, for example, our relationship, our
    career, our life or the welfare of the Universe.

5. *Learning*

We clarify the wisdom and any benefits we or others may have acquired as a result of the hurt and assess how this can be used to help us and/or others.

If these sound a daunting package of tasks, remember that, unlike a Government Enquiry, our Perspective work can sometimes be done in less than a minute. And very rarely is it appropriate or necessary to do all the tasks with each hurt. Indeed, sometimes you may only need to do one of them.

You have probably already automatically done most of these tasks yourself when encountering various small hurts. This next exercise should demonstrate just how much of a Perspective expert you already are!

Instant Exercise: Spot Simple Perspective in Action

Identify and name some of the Perspective tasks which are being carried out during a few seconds of self-talk in these examples. Notice that not all the tasks are appropriate in every situation (answers at the end of the chapter):

1. Jim was disappointed at losing a game and said to himself, 'It's only a game after all . . . and we had some fun. I've won many times before and probably will again. It's good for my soul to lose occasionally.'

2. Chris was annoyed at being let down by a colleague who cancelled an important meeting at the last minute because 'a more important priority' had emerged. After a little swearing he said to himself, 'Well, at least this cancellation wasn't my fault. And he apologized profusely and will feel guilty. That means that I may

have a better chance of persuading him. Now I have a little more time to get those statistics.'

3. Francesca had her handbag stolen and said to herself, 'I suppose this is the price you pay for having a holiday in the heart of a city surrounded by so much poverty. Well, they didn't stab you, like they did Carole when she was mugged. That bag was getting shabby anyway and needed replacing. I must stop going down streets like that on my own – after all, this is not the first time this has happened to me.'

4. Robert, on hearing of a great uncle's death, said to himself, 'Oh, I will miss him. I enjoyed so much being able to pop in to see him when I was passing through Durham. But at least he lived life to the full and he was not alone when he died. It was good that I managed to see him not so long ago and took that great photo of his ever-present smile. It'll be a reminder of his "Keep looking on the bright side" philosophy which always buoyed me up.'

Some of you will of course have identified with these examples more readily than others. As I mentioned earlier, Perspective comes all too easily to those who are naturally inclined to think analytically. It also comes more easily to those who, like Robert's relative, are lucky enough to be born optimists and bounce-backers. But to those amongst us who have had an excessive number of hurts or been through a major trauma, the Perspective tasks may represent a real challenge. So if you are one of the latter, I suggest that you do a little preparatory work before attempting to do the Perspective Questionnaire on pages 151–5. It will energize the parts of your brain that you need to use and put you into a helpful open mindset.

PREPARATORY WORK TO HELP YOU MAKE THE BEST OF PERSPECTIVE

1. Wake Up Your Mind

Perspective tasks require a good degree of mental agility and optimism. We need to switch easily from left-brain work for analysis into a right-brain view to see the Big Picture. We are also required to attempt to understand a variety of perceptions and beliefs, so this task also requires flexible thinking. Finally, we need to access our creative thinking powers in order to extract the learning and positive benefits.

As we have already discussed, after very many hurts our minds don't function as well as they usually do. And although yours should be working a good deal better by this stage, it still may be on the sluggish side. Many people find that when they are faced with the Perspective tasks, their thoughts have a tendency to either circle around in their heads or become stuck in a rut of negativity (such as dwelling on pessimistic 'what if . . .' or 'if only . . .' scenarios). This is why I suggest that you do some simple mind warm-up exercises first. These will help you to do the main Perspective Questionnaire (pages 151–5) so much more quickly and thoroughly.

Brain Gym

These quick physical exercises stimulate the connections between the right and left hemispheres of the brain, and are a great help if you are stuck in a thinking rut. (I use them for writing blocks.) Do them every morning for a week or so before you start the Perspective Questionnaire if you are dealing with a major trauma.

- March vigorously on the spot for three minutes (lifting right leg and left arm and vice-versa).

- Working from right to left, use your arm to draw a large imaginary figure of eight lying on its side in front of you. Then immediately go backwards drawing one from left to right. Repeat three times.

- Put your right hand behind you and bring your left leg up to meet it so that your fingers and toes touch. Do the same immediately with your left hand and right leg. Repeat six times as quickly as your ability to balance will allow.

Brainstorm

This is a highly acclaimed method of starting off a creative thinking exercise. If it is not familiar to you, practise using it by choosing a subject unrelated to your hurt.

Put the key word in the centre of a very large piece of paper (A1 or large piece of old wallpaper) – as in the illustration opposite. Stare at this word for a few moments and then, as quickly as possible, throw down on to the page any other words that come into your head. Don't worry about being sensible (or even polite!).

Mind Map

Using your brainstorm of your hurt, begin to organize your thoughts using the Mind Map technique similar to the one opposite.

Brainstorm

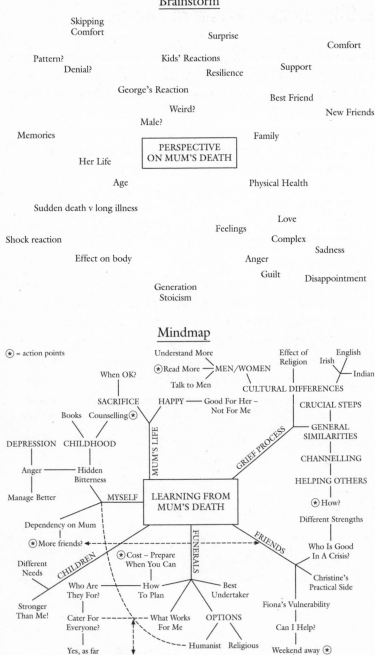

Skipping
Comfort

Surprise

Comfort

Pattern?

Kids' Reactions

Support

Denial?

Resilience

George's Reaction

Best Friend

Weird?

New Friends

Male?

Memories

Family

PERSPECTIVE
ON MUM'S DEATH

Her Life

Age

Physical Health

Sudden death v long illness

Love

Feelings

Complex

Shock reaction

Sadness

Effect on body

Anger

Guilt

Disappointment

Generation
Stoicism

Mindmap

(*) = action points

Understand More

Effect of   English
Religion   Irish

(*)Read More — MEN/WOMEN

Indian

When OK?

Talk to Men

CULTURAL DIFFERENCES

SACRIFICE   HAPPY — Good For Her –
                         Not For Me

CRUCIAL STEPS

Books Counselling(*)

GENERAL
SIMILARITIES

DEPRESSION CHILDHOOD

CHANNELLING

Anger ———— Hidden
                  Bitterness

HELPING OTHERS

Manage Better

(*) How?

MYSELF

Different Strengths

Dependency on Mum

(*)More friends? ◄- -

Who Is Good
In A Crisis?

Different
Needs

(*)Cost – Prepare
When You Can

Christine's
Practical Side

Stronger
Than Me!

Who Are   How
They For?   To Plan

Best
Undertaker

Fiona's Vulnerability

Cater For - - -
Everyone?

What Works
For Me

OPTIONS

Can I Help?

Yes, as far
as possible COMPROMISE!(*)

Humanist Religious

Weekend away (*)
together later

MUM'S LIFE

GRIEF PROCESS

LEARNING FROM
MUM'S DEATH

FUNERALS

FRIENDS

CHILDREN

2. Stimulate a Positive Mood

These suggestions are designed to help lift your spirits and help you to think more energetically and positively. If they don't work for you, use your own tricks or ask some persistently happy friends to share theirs.

- Watch a comedy programme or video every night for a week.

- Buy yourself a book of humorous quotations or jokes and dip into it each morning for five minutes before getting out of bed. Do the same before going to sleep.

- Eat at least one portion of delicious sensuous food each day. This is a tip from Bob Ayling, a famous and highly successful British businessman. When being interviewed about how he fought back from his innumerable setbacks, he said, 'You can't be miserable for long eating strawberries.'

- Force yourself to smile as often as you can. Research has shown that doing this actually stimulates the production of the brain chemicals known as endorphins, which trigger pleasurable emotions.

- Beg, buy or borrow a book of quotations specifically designed for healing.

- Use the GEE strategy below. It is designed to switch you out of the irrational thinking state that frequently accompanies an emotional hurt.

The GEE Strategy

This strategy works as a quick fix for breaking out of a negative thinking rut.

The moment you are aware of making a negative statement, ask yourself the following three simple questions. These will switch you back into a rational (rather than an emotional) thinking mode. The person in the following example was a twice-divorced father of two who had become emotionally hurt and dispirited by being turned down by three women he had approached for a second date. In each category there are two statements. The first is his immediate, emotional reaction to events, and the second gives a more rational approach.

1. Am I **G**eneralizing from one or a few specific experiences? For example:

   'It's my own stupid fault. I always choose the wrong type. That's just me. I can't blame anyone else.'
   → 'I have actually only had two bites of the cherry . . . I was only eighteen with the first and then rushed in too quickly before healing with the second. Jane was too young to know her own mind as well. Fiona knew what she was taking on with the kids, even if we did marry before it had been well tested out.'

2. Am I **E**xaggerating current problems, potential hazards or difficulties? For example:

   'If I get so upset now over being turned down for a few dates, I would have a complete breakdown if another marriage didn't work out.'
   → 'I haven't been so upset that I couldn't continue working and looking after the kids. I

have only made three attempts – the dating agency has thousands of women on its books and I have only been a member for a month. Anyway, if I have another failed marriage at least I now know how to recover, so even if I am hurt I will survive.'

3. Am I **E**xcluding any positive aspects or potential? For example:

'No woman today wants a man who has been divorced twice and is burdened with two kids.'
➤ 'There are women who have been divorced twice themselves. There are also many who will appreciate a man who now knows what he needs and what he is looking for. And they can see for themselves how committed a father I am. My kids are fantastic company and I wouldn't be without them. I am quite capable of looking after them myself – they could be an asset to the right woman, not a burden.'

3. Challenge Your Beliefs

Perspective needs a very open mind. When we are hurt (and therefore feeling vulnerable) we feel more secure in the company of familiar beliefs, attitudes and values. This not only includes the ones in our own head, but it also includes external ones too. We will have a tendency to steer ourselves towards people who share our core value system. We might seek out their company or just listen more intently to their point of view. You have probably seen an example of this when witnessing a scene in a public place similar to the following.

It was a usual busy Monday morning on a main-line London station. A belligerent-looking group of young lads started threatening a guard who wouldn't let them through the train barrier (I assume they didn't have the right ticket). The exchange became very heated and then physically violent. A passenger intervened and was thrown to the ground and sworn at.

While waiting for the transport police to arrive, people started huddling into a group around the scene. I watched them quickly sort themselves into like-minded discussion pairs and groups. With my well-honed eavesdropping skills, I heard a variety of 'Isn't it awful . . . I blame . . .' conversations:

> *'I blame the parents – they should be locked up. Youth of today have no respect . . . and there's no discipline in schools.'*
> *'Nowhere is safe these days . . . We are too soft in this country . . . there should be more police on the stations . . . you don't see this happening in Germany. I lived there for . . .'*
> *'I was queuing 20 minutes for a ticket and my patience was running thin too . . . yes, they are asking for trouble only having two ticket windows open for this crowd . . . They said they had three people off sick, but it's always this bad.'*

This was an example of poor Perspective in action. The passengers who had witnessed this scene felt vicariously hurt. (As London Transport is constantly under threat from terrorism, any scene such as this immediately ignites the collective fear-and-hurt button. This immediately brings the infamously solitary London passengers together.)

In sharing their theories about the responsibility for this incident, the crowd were leaping straight forward to a poor version of Perspective (instead of first Exploring together, talking about what had just happened, Expressing their fear and Comforting each other). In taking this premature healing leap, they carried with them their prejudices (which have their roots in fear). These were then collectively reinforced by the sharing amongst like-minded others. So it is unlikely that positive outcomes resulted from this experience – indeed more fear, mistrust and cynicism is likely to have grown.

But who hasn't been tempted to fall into this kind of false Perspective response? It immediately makes us feel a little safer as we become part of the crowd and therefore stronger than when we were standing alone. But the good news is that once we are at this stage, we can get just the same feeling from engaging in the following kinds of Perspective tasks:

- When talking to others who have had the same experience, look out in particular for people who have had different reactions to yours. Listen and ask questions to try to understand their point of view and why they may see it from a different Perspective. Remember that now is the time for listening and taking note of what *others* felt and believed might have happened and why.

- Meet, hear and read about people in these kinds of situations who have had the same hurt, but a more dramatic version of it. But be careful not to dismiss your own as 'nothing'. I know how tempting this can be. When I was at this stage in healing from my loss of Laura, I found my attention wandering to stories about major disasters in which parents lost all their children. I had to fight away the thoughts on the theme that I was 'lucky'. But, on balance, I still think that this kind of thinking about people who have had to cope with even more than I did, helped me with gaining Perspective and provided energizing fuel for me when I moved on to our first bonus stage in this strategy – Constructive Channelling.

- Join a self-help or pressure group. But watch out for the ones that are just stuck in a moaning and groaning rut. If there isn't an appropriate one in your area, think about starting a small one. You can do this with just two to three people. Your local council may well provide you with accommodation and a small grant to do this. Sometimes they will also provide a leader to kick-start the group. If not, rotate the leadership. But try to make sure that you have some ground rules to stop some people dominating. This can happen so easily when people are still not sufficiently recovered from their hurt.

- Read widely on the subject. Do a search on the internet for free information, but you may also need a few books to obtain a balanced view. Ask a bookseller or librarian for help. Many self-help groups have a reading list. So might your doctor. (I have only just discovered myself that in the UK most NHS trusts have reading lists and many of my books have been on these for a long time!)

- When doing your research, try to find out how your hurt is viewed and dealt with in other countries. There are well-known differences, for example, between many countries on the subjects of infidelity, corporal punishment of children and respect for the elderly and disabled. Debating these can be very enlightening and challenging and, of course, healing.

- Look out for survivor stories in films, magazines and in TV and radio shows. The latter sometimes include phone-ins and so will also give you an opportunity to debate a little.

- Become an internet blogger or chatter. You don't know how to do that? Ask an internet buff. In short, it is a way of airing and sharing news and views on an internet website. It is a good idea to choose ones which are moderated to ensure that the debates are not offensive, libellous or dangerous.

- Play Devil's Advocate with yourself. Set two chairs opposite one another and have an argument by

changing from one chair to the other. Select radically
different points of view for each chair. You can do
this to expand your thoughts on several of the
Perspective task areas.

• If appropriate, ask other people for feedback on your
reaction to the hurt and also for any thoughts on
your responsibility for any aspect of it. Be careful
whom you ask. They should be people who
genuinely want to help you recover and learn from
the experience. They should also be confident
enough to be honest and know how to give negative
feedback in a constructive way.

4. Feast on Humble Pie

When we are emotionally hurt we become egocentric. This is
another of our auto-survival responses. We need to be super-self-
focussed in order to go through the healing stages that we have
done so far. It is a time when we also may have received much more
attention than usual from others. But obviously if this me-me focus
persists, it will become counter-productive. We will lose friends fast
and will be less able to live and work within society. (Isn't it true
that in today's world, most of us share the expectation that mutual
satisfaction of needs is a key requirement for a successful friendship, community or commercial relationship?)

Perspective requires us to have a sense of proportion about our
own importance in both our micro and macro-worlds. The aim
of eating a little humble pie before you start is to help you
re-establish a more balanced view of your own importance. Here
are ways that I and others have achieved this, but you may well
have your favourite 'back-to-earth' technique.

• Walking in the countryside where there are vast open
green spaces (such as the moors in England);

- Walking along a beach or sailing a boat on the sea;

- Gazing at stars. This can be done by a visit to a planetarium or staring at a night sky which is relatively free from light pollution;

- Taking a holiday or visit to an historic place such as Stonehenge in England or (if you still need some extra compensation!), treating yourself to a more exotic location such as Machu Piccu in Peru or the Pyramids in Egypt. If your budget or diary prevents you from making a longer trip, a visit to a museum or a dip into a few travel or history books would do;

- Visiting a community where people have a lower standard of living than you do. Clients on my courses in Spain have often commented that spending time in the rural village where we worked helped them achieve Perspective. If you cannot do a real-life visit, you can achieve the same effect from reading novels or watching films;

- Seeing, hearing or reading the work of highly successful and talented people in any field that interests you such as an aspect of business, art, dance or sport;

- Visiting a charitable institution where dedicated and altruistic people are working voluntarily or for next-to-nothing.

Now that you have put yourself in the right frame of mind, it is time for some serious solitary reflection. In the following questionnaire exercise you will find a series of questions to help you achieve the five Perspective tasks. You may find that not all the questions are relevant to the hurt that you are currently working on. But, for the purposes of learning about the process, do at least consider each one. You could try applying the questions to a past hurt or to a hypothetical one.

The Perspective Questionnaire

I. Context

? What was going on inside my head at the time? Was I thinking about anything in particular that could be relevant? Was I happy or sad?

Note: Remember, hurts don't necessarily always hit hardest if you are already feeling down. Being in an intense state of joy can make a hurt feel even more painful than it normally would. For example, a few months ago, I was walking around the stunningly beautiful *Feria del Caballo* (annual fair) in Jerez, Spain, and commented to my husband how lucky I was to be there and to be with someone I loved. A second later, my phone alerted me to a text message which gave me some seriously disappointing news. This intrusion of negativity had the effect of killing stone-dead my positive mood and, as a result, I felt even more upset than perhaps I would otherwise have done. I suspect this is true as every time I told this story to friends, I have emphasized the context.

? What was going on in my external world at the time? Was the environment pleasant or stressful?

Note: Hearing the news that your house has been broken into may bring more or less pain depending on where you are at the time. You may react differently to the news if you are on holiday rather than in a war zone or in a highly stressful work environment.

? Were there any people around? Was anyone else hurt besides me? If so, was I affected by their reactions?

Note: The degree to which other people were upset, shocked or angry can affect how we feel. Think of players in a tennis match. The hurt they feel at a defeat in one game can be intensified by booing from the crowd. It can dampen their spirits to the extent that they lose the next game as well.

2. Patterns

? Have I felt hurt in a similar way before? If so, how often? And when was the first?

Note: The deep pang of isolation that John, a client, felt when his girlfriend broke off their engagement was evocative of the time when his friend and colleague moved to Australia. It also reminded him of the feeling of social isolation he felt when he was not chosen as cox for the university rowing team which he had been part of for three years.

? Were there any similarities between my internal state and what happened? If so, what were they?

Note: Each time the above happened to John he was approaching a transition in his life. So he was losing external support while he was internally stressed and worried.

? Were the people who were involved or around similar or did they behave in a similar fashion?

Note: All the people around John on each occasion were people he loved deeply and with whom he shared fun times. This made the last disconnection from his girlfriend much harder because he began to think (albeit irrationally) that '. . . *this always happens to me when I get really close to people.*'

3. Responsibility

?Did any aspect of my personality or my behaviour have a bearing on what happened?

Note: Several years after the break-up of my first marriage, I could see that my own blind determination to give my children the happy, secure childhood that I did not have myself may have been a reason why I did not notice the obvious (with hindsight) signs that my first husband was leading a double life.

?Was anyone else partly or wholly responsible?

Note: Understanding do-gooders like me can have a field day answering this question. We have to take care not to find so many different people to blame that there is no share of responsibility left for the main perpetrator!

?Were any other factors partly to blame?

Note: Take care not to find many of these (such as the weather, economic strain, generation gap, hormones, illness, lack of education, etc.) that you start to feel overly compassionate for any irresponsible or calculatingly selfish people in control of these factors.

4. Significance

?On a scale of one to ten, how serious an impact did this hurt have on me and my life?

Note: It may help to compare this hurt to other emotional wounds you or others have experienced.

? Does this hurt have any importance in relation to anyone else?

Note: It could have indirectly impacted children, colleagues, clients, friends, etc.

? Does this hurt have significance in relation to any wider issue which is of concern for me?

Note: Look at the experience in the light of other issues such as the rights of women/children/senior citizens; medical ethics; religious beliefs, etc.

5. Learning

? Have I learned anything about myself as a result of this hurt and its effects?

Note: Ask yourself, for example: Am I less assertive/independent than I need to be?; Am I overly trusting or needy of other's approval?; Have I loved him/her/it more than even *I* thought I did? Can I both love and dislike the same person?; Do I need more good friends in my life?; Do I need to work/revise/prepare harder if I want to make the grade? Have I learned anything about anyone else?
Note: It could be, for example, that the experience has shown you that he or she does not share the same values/expectations/life dreams as you.

? Have I learned anything about life in general?

Note: You may, for example, have become more aware of a need to live life well, as you don't know when it will end. Alternatively, it may help you to accept that life isn't fair. (This is what many of my daughter Laura's friends said they had gained from her death.)

? Is there anything I can do to protect myself from re-experiencing such a hurt?

Note: You may make a resolution that in future you will use your head to judge whether your heart is pulling you in the right direction, or that you must always have a Plan B ready and waiting;

? Have I grown as a person in any way as a result of this hurt?

Note: As a result of what has happened you could judge that you are now more emotionally resilient/humble/knowledgeable about people; more empathic with people who are vulnerable or rejected; aware that there is a vengeful or murderously angry side of you which needs controlling.

? Have there been any benefits to anyone or anything else?

Note: Perhaps your children/colleagues/friends have seen what has happened to you and learned. Or maybe the people who comforted you gained in self-esteem and know they can rest assured that they can depend on you for help if ever they need it.

I hope that you found doing this exercise enlightening. It could be useful to try to summarize your answers in the form of a very short story. This would be one that you could relate to other people whenever you need or want to talk about your hurt.

TIME FOR 'CLOSURE'?

'Closure' is a term that is now commonly used to describe the experience of coming to an emotional conclusion after a difficult life event. It often involves acting out some kind of ritual, but it can be doing anything which gives you a sense of conclusion. The purpose of closure is to be able to move on.

My experience is that if the healing process has progressed along the lines I am suggesting with this strategy, closure happens naturally. A feeling of achieving a conclusion usually accompanies Perspective, but sometimes it doesn't happen immediately. Sometimes it happens after one or both of the following two bonus stages that we are going to look at next.

But if you are the kind of person for whom rituals work, it would certainly do no harm to do them at any time after finishing Perspective. I have often done these ritualistic kinds of closure with clients when I am working with groups. They can then produce a close sense of bonding which is usually translated into invaluable practical and emotional support during the early challenging stages of moving on. The suggestions of what we should do always come from the clients themselves. It is important that you do what feels right for you and is fitting for the particular hurt you have had. But to get you thinking about what might be possible, here are a few examples of closure rituals that have worked for people whom I know;

- Clearing out a deceased person's house or room and having a farewell drink in their honour;

- Holding a memorial service (if it is not too soon after the death. A funeral is always too soon as you would not have healed);

- A ceremony to accompany the scattering of the ashes;

- Having a memorial concert;

- Writing an account and evaluation of the experience (a longer version of the story I suggested earlier). Then, having it bound or put in a file and put on *your* bookshelf (or in the cellar if you have one);

- Creating a piece of art work that is for you (not for anyone else as you might do in Channelling);

- Writing down the negative aspects of the experience and tearing them up, burning and burying the ashes or scattering them at sea or on a river or mountainside;

- Tearing up photos or papers, newspaper cuttings and doing as above;

- Paying a final farewell visit to treasured places. When I was upset about having to leave Yorkshire, which had been my home for seventeen years, I spent a day visiting my favourite locations on my own and saying goodbye;

- Buying a beautiful casket in which to store positive memorabilia;

- Compiling an album of photos depicting the happy times together after healing from a divorce or separation.

PERSPECTIVE IN A NUTSHELL

To examine the experience of the hurt from a Big Picture point of view with the aim of gaining a sense of conclusion and taking something positive from it to help you move on, you will need to:

- Look at the context in which the hurt occurred.

- Identify any familiar patterns.

- Judge where responsibility lies.

- Assess its true significance.

- Acknowledge the learning you have gained.

- Perform a closure ritual if appropriate.

Answers to exercise on pages 138–9

1. Jim was disappointed at losing a game and said to himself, 'It's only a game after all . . . and we had some fun. (**Learning**) I've won many times before and probably will again. (**Significance**) It's good for my soul to lose occasionally.' (**Learning**)
2. Chris was annoyed at being let down by a colleague who cancelled an important meeting at the last minute because 'a more important priority' had emerged. After a little swearing he said to himself, 'Well, at least this cancellation wasn't my fault. (**Responsibility**) And he apologized profusely and will feel guilty. That means that I may have a better chance of persuading him. Now I have a little more time to get those statistics.' (**Learning**)
3. Francesca had her handbag stolen and said to herself, 'I suppose this is the price you pay for having a holiday in the heart of a city surrounded by so much poverty. (**Context** and **Responsibility**) Well, they didn't stab you, like they did Carole when she was mugged. That bag was getting shabby anyway and needed replacing. (**Significance**) I must stop going down streets like that on my own – after all this is not the first time this has happened to me.' (**Patterns** and **Learning**)
4. Robert, on hearing of a great-uncle's death, said to himself, 'Oh, I will miss him. I enjoyed so much being able to pop in to see him when I was passing through Durham. But at least he lived life to the full and he was not alone when he died. It was good that I managed to see him not so long ago and took that great photo of his ever-present smile. (**Context**) It'll be a reminder to me of his "Keep looking on the bright side" philosophy which always buoyed me up.' (**Learning**)

6. Channelling

Well, here we are at last! We have arrived at my own most comfortable healing spot! I am one of the world's experts on Channelling. I started practising it in infancy and I am doing it right now as I write this book.

As we shall discuss later, there are innumerable ways to Channel. Essentially, they all involve doing one or more of the following:

- Using the learning from our hurt to help ourselves;

- Using the learning to help others;

- Directing the renewed energy we gained from healing into building, creating, growing or producing something which will benefit our community or the world in a positive way.

Channelling, as you already know, is a bonus healing stage. Although we don't, strictly speaking, *need* it, I can highly recommend it. When we are able to do it we feel extra healed and extra strengthened and more often than not, our Channelling benefits others as well. Throughout history, it has been the driving force behind many highly successful individuals, pressure groups, charities, books, plays and films. Let's look at a few famous examples:

Simon Wiesenthal was a survivor of the Nazi death camps. He dedicated his life to documenting the crimes of the Holocaust and to hunting down the perpetrators.

Nelson Mandela was a political prisoner for 26 years. Together with his fellow inmates he set up a powerful awareness-raising museum in Robben Island. Now aged 89, he still uses his fame and wisdom to support charities and diplomatic efforts to resolve conflict.

Madonna fought to gain the part of Evita in the film about the Argentinean legend because so much of Eva Peron's story resembled her own early life struggles, as well as her ultimate success. Although the film met with a mixed critical reception (as she must have known it would) she was obviously motivated to do it for emotional healing reasons.

Picasso painted his anti-war picture 'Guernica' in response to his and his country's emotional hurts during the Spanish Civil War and the dictatorship of Franco. Picasso refused to allow the painting to return to Spain until certain human rights conditions were met.

Harold Pinter wrote his famous play *Betrayal* after the hurtful break-up of his first marriage.

Isabel Allende had to go into exile in Venezuela with her husband and children after the overthrow and assassination in 1973 of her uncle, Salvador Allende, president of Chile. She has set up a foundation which awards prizes to organizations dedicated to resolving conflict without violence. When her daughter was diagnosed with terminal cancer she wrote her extraordinary book *Paula*.

Christopher Reeve was paralysed by a horse-riding accident and used his Superman fame to start a charity to fund research and help others with the same condition. He wrote an inspirational autobiography entitled *Still Me*.

Oprah Winfrey was raped as a child. She uses the power of her famous programme to support anti-rape causes.

K'Naan Award is a multi-award-winning rap artist who escaped from Somalia at the age of thirteen. He now writes and sings songs to raise awareness of the problems in his country.

Kylie Minogue developed breast cancer and is now a benefactor and campaigner for the Breast Cancer Care charity. She recently donated $13,860 to them – the price she gained for auctioning one of her bras!

Simon Weston is a Falklands veteran who received 49 per cent burns when 22 of his 30-strong platoon were killed. He uses his inspirational survivor story to help raise money for his charity, Weston Spirit, which provides personal development programmes for young people.

George Eliot's great novel *Middlemarch* was based on her own experiences of marriage problems and frustration with society's limiting expectations for women.

Stephen Harris is the rock star of Guns 'n' Roses and drug-addiction fame. He is now doing a medical degree 'while I still have time to do some good'.

With so many inspirational role models as well as its obvious benefits, is it any wonder that many people share with me a tendency to jump prematurely into Channelling?

I found myself doing this only the other day. Building work on our new house in Spain had been suddenly stopped by officials from the local town hall. We were apparently building a wall that was a small number of centimetres closer to our boundary wall than the law permitted. Everyone I have spoken with about this decision thinks that this is an absurd application of the letter of the law as our boundary wall only backs on to some unusable scrubland. As it means another few months without a kitchen, plus spending a substantial extra sum of money, I was extremely upset and frustrated. But interestingly, one of my first thoughts was, 'I must write an article to warn other naïve newcomers about Spanish building law.'

This kind of instant leap over all the essential stages of healing is common for people like me for whom Channelling has become such a way of life and so integral to their personality. It feels normal and sensible and, because it is associated with healing in our minds, we do find it initially calming. But at the time of the hurt, we may think we are being purely altruistic or inspired. If you were brave enough to challenge us 'saints' about our motivation, we would become defensive. We might vehemently protest that it has nothing to do with healing our hurt; we truly believe we have merely been inspired by seeing a need.

Some expert Channellers even make a conscious and unashamed choice to jump straight to this stage. They may argue that it is an efficient and rapid way to recuperate after a hurt. They say it distracts from the pain, turns a setback into an opportunity and is better than self-pity. This kind of argument is constantly being reinforced by our mass media culture. Almost daily the press encourages a grieving person to recount their hurt immediately after a personal or national disaster in order to 'help others'. The temptation to co-operate is understandably too hard to resist. Everyone knows the power of press coverage to kick-start a pressure group or a fund-raising campaign and that this has to be harnessed while the public are still in a state of empathy prompted by the shock. I have fallen into this trap myself.

Within 24 hours of my daughter Laura's death, I had decided to set up a foundation in her name. The aim of our Foundation was to help other young people find and develop the confidence to pursue their life-dream. It was an excellent Channelling project for me. Let me explain why. Laura had recently decided to leave her university course as she felt it was not right for her. Although she knew her decision was clearly correct, she fell into a state of despair about the prospect of ever finding any career that would suit her. Luckily, I had been able to drop my own work for a few months and spend time helping her to rebuild her self-confidence and explore and establish a new life-dream. The Foundation offered me the chance to use everything I had learned through this experience to help other young people and gain the personal satisfaction of seeing the results that I had been denied by Laura's tragic early death.

As I already had some media presence and Laura had also been on national TV with me talking about confidence and young people, I was approached fairly immediately by a considerable number of journalists. I saw my participation in interviews as an invaluable way to promote the Foundation.

The result was that the work of the Foundation grew much too quickly for my own emotional health and for the good of the organization we were building. I allowed ideas that were too ambitious for our limited resources to be put into practice and I made some unwise decisions about the staffing of the projects. In short, my heart was ruling my head and pushing me to run a marathon when I was still too unfit to walk. Fortunately (thanks again to my work in this field), I realized what was happening in time to do a rescue operation. I passed the hands-on work, administration and PR to others and just played a supportive role. In the meantime, I backtracked to the point in my healing journey where I needed to be. The result was that the Foundation went on to do some excellent groundbreaking work and I recovered my own emotional equilibrium.

This personal experience greatly reinforced my belief that Channelling must be seen as bonus healing. Unless we are emotionally stable and resilient, there is a danger that Channelling won't be as effective and constructive as it has the potential to be. It can also have a detrimental effect on the hurt person and those whom they so passionately want to help. Of course I should have known better, I had seen plenty of evidence of this happening in my career in the field of self-help and mental health advocacy. And, of course, I had already devised the strategy. But because my emotional cut was so very deep, my previous psychological programming overrode my rational educated mind.

WHAT FACTORS CAN CREATE AN INSTANT CHANNELLER?

Once again my own personal story illustrates some of the most common causes. If you are a Channeller, you will identify with some of the key factors, consequences and solutions. I have highlighted these in bold for those who are not yet so expert in this field.

As I have already mentioned, my Channelling habits started early. So early, in fact, that I think my **genetic inheritance** has set me up to excel naturally at this stage of healing. I have been a pragmatic and practical person for as long as I can remember. In addition, I also undoubtedly inherited a good dose of Channelling potential from the artists and pioneers in my father's family background. And, although I know very little about my mother's family, I do know that she was a nurse and considered to be exceptionally good at her healing duties. (The helping professions attract natural Channellers.)

Perhaps my **role in my family reinforced this natural inclination**. And being the first child in the family also played its part. Most of the few early memories I do have are of trying to **protect and help** my younger brother and sister from the pain and suffering caused by our mother's alcoholism. As you already know, I have very few recollections of my early childhood, but I do have one clear memory of my toddling brother (eighteen months younger than me) standing at the top of the stairs with tears in his eyes, listening to the frightening exchanges taking place downstairs between my parents. I recall dragging him into the bedroom, reassuring him and singing nursery rhymes to get him to go back to sleep. (Poor boy – I sing in very flat tones!) Then, as I remember, I stood guard at the top of the stairs for what seemed like hours until I was spotted by my father.

Throughout the rest of my childhood I continued to Channel. In the children's homes, **my behaviour was continually held up as an example of helpfulness and caring and so these behaviours were further reinforced**. (Although little did the staff know that, at night, I was the secret leader of another kind of Channelling activity. I created and led a secret society that indulged in dancing and picnicking well into the night. Our badges, candles and other gear are possibly still buried under those floorboards!)

With hindsight, my choice of a **Channelling career path** in the helping professions was fairly predictable. After an early flirtation with the vision of becoming a missionary nun (I was largely convent educated), I had the unrealistic ambition to reform the world as a director of documentary drama films. When that dream had to be abandoned, I became a social worker and later a drama-therapist and self-help author.

In my early career, my Channelling was not always constructively helpful. For example, as a Child Care Officer it was my duty to see that children were safe within their family environment and, if they were not, to arrange for them to be taken into care. **My driving passion was to make sure others did not get hurt in the way I had been**. I wanted to keep children out of children's homes as this had been such an unhappy experience for me. However, **my keenness to do this sometimes blinded me to the reality** of parental abuse and as a result, there were some serious consequences for a child of one family. This child was badly battered by the father while I was on holiday and I had not considered there was enough risk to warrant someone checking in my absence. The father was given a custodial sentence and the children taken into care.

Later, working as a housemother in a children's home, my **emotional need** to make life 'happy' for my charges meant that I was quite **unable to maintain discipline and make necessary tough decisions for fear of upsetting people**. As a result, the older children continually bullied and hurt the younger ones and the home was badly managed.

While my well-meaning efforts at work were causing some destructive consequences for others and becoming exhausting and dispiriting for me, a similar negative Channelling pattern was taking place in my personal life. I had become **overly preoccupied with saving the world and my social life suffered. On the**

personal relationship front, I was equally busy rescuing the lost souls whom I chose for friends and lovers.

So my early adult Channelling was setting me up for failure on all fronts. I was continually driven to work on problems that were beyond my power to do anything constructive about. It wasn't until a **dark depression** drove me to a serious suicide attempt that I realized that there was something psychologically wrong with me! Previously, I had just thought the world was rotten and I was a miserable failure. It took some heavy confrontation from psychiatrists to make me realize that it was the mass of **unhealed hurt from my childhood experiences that was at the root of my destructive Channelling habits.**

But my story of Channelling disasters does have a happy ending! After receiving therapy and **doing some considerable healing work**, I became even more motivated to continue my Channelling career. However, the difference was that I did by then have many years of well-supervised professional psychotherapy training behind me. As a result, I became very much **more self-aware and self-disciplined** in my work. This meant that I could begin to use my Channelling skills constructively. I grew to love my work even more as I was able to do it with very much greater success. In the arena of my personal and social life I have also become much more disciplined. I have learned to say 'no' and to **conserve and apportion my compassion carefully** so that I have enough time and energy for the relationships that matter most to me.

If any aspects of my story have rung bells for you, you too may be a Channeller by nature and/or nurture. This means that you will need to take extra care to check that you are in emotionally good-enough shape to do Channelling in a constructive way. To help you do this I have compiled a list of warning signals below. If you notice that you are experiencing any of the following, take time out to reflect. Show the list to your nearest and dearest and ask them to keep an eye out for any of these signals as well. You don't necessarily have to give up your Channelling projects, but you may need to put them on hold or delegate them until you have backtracked as far as you need down the healing path.

WARNING SIGNALS OF PREMATURE CHANNELLING

Stop to think when you are feeling:

- **Compelled at all costs**. Unhealed Channellers often say 'I just *have to* do it' or 'I know it is silly but I *must* continue.' Sometimes, this urge is likened to a 'calling' or a vocation. Outsiders may point out that they are failing abysmally to achieve their goal, but they continue to ignore this reality and are often prepared to 'martyr' themselves to their cause. (This is commonly seen in badly supervised charity projects which are destined for bankruptcy or are being abused by their clients.)

- **Personally hurt when your offers of help are continually rejected**. (This is common in a relationship where one party who has been to counselling is on a mission to help the other sort themselves out.)

- **Angry and frustrated when people return to their 'old ways' after receiving so much help from you**. (This is common when volunteers work with persistent self-harmers, offenders or drug abusers.)

- **Cynical and despairing when your reforming projects repeatedly fail**. (This is commonly felt among some political activists.)

- **That you are the one and only person who can solve the problem or do the job**. (This grandiosity is a familiar trait in professional do-gooders who often then become sufferers from 'burn-out' stress.)

- **That your work on a creative project becomes obsessional and you feel that others do not**

appreciate its importance or your need to do it perfectly. (Unhealed artists working on highly personal and emotionally laden work often feel continually dissatisfied with their results even when critics rave about them and they sell for a fortune. Beethoven regarded his 'Moonlight Sonata' as an 'inferior' piece, even though it was enormously popular; Edvard Grieg was dissatisfied with his acclaimed *Peer Gynt* suite.)

- **A passionate and obsessive desire to ensure someone is punished or shamed**. (This is an understandable desire, for example, for people whose children have been abused. This may be a highly desirable and justly deserved side-outcome, but it should not be your prime motivator. Channelling is essentially a positive healing process for you and a constructive way to help prevent others from becoming hurt. Let others do the punitive work if it needs to be done.)

- **Bursts of unexpected and uncontrollable irritation or temper**. (This is common for people who have had a severe traumatic hurt that will at some level be a wound that could be re-opened for the rest of their lives. If this happens, backtrack to the appropriate healing stage and later, if you want to Channel, choose a low-stress project. Leave the big Channelling challenges to those who have been less hurt than you have been.)

- **Physical or mental symptoms of stress**. (These could be, for example, headaches, sleeplessness, eating difficulties, lack of concentration, phobias or anxiety attacks. If these occur, follow the same path as I have suggested above.)

That's quite enough about Channelling problems for me and probably you too! Let's return to its undoubted positive potential.

POSITIVE EFFECTS OF CHANNELLING

When Channelling is done by emotionally stable and resilient people, it is the greatest wonder of the psychological world. I'd challenge anyone to convince me that there is any activity that is more satisfying, uplifting and self-esteem building than that which transforms a hurtful experience into a powerfully positive force that can help others as well as yourself. We have already looked at famous examples of how some people have managed to do just this; now let's look at some more everyday ways to Channel that we ordinary mortals can use.

Raising Awareness of a Related Issue

This works very well if you think a social change could prevent your hurt being repeated on others. Nina Bawden, who became a widow as a result of the Potter's Bar rail disaster in the UK, joined the campaign to help the victims prove that it had been entirely avoidable. I recently heard a radio interview with a man whose brother was killed in an accident as a result of someone using a mobile phone while driving. He is heading up a community campaign on the Isle of Wight to stop people using handsets whilst driving.

The most powerful way of raising awareness is to tell your story rather than just preach at people. When appropriate, you could also write to the press, MPs, relevant charities and other organizations, or join in a radio or TV phone-in. The research you did for Perspective should help you, but you may need to do a little more and/or seek professional advice if the subject is contentious or may backfire legally on you.

Befriending Lonely and Needy People

This is a useful way of plugging a hole in your heart if you have lost someone or people close to you because you have moved, a relationship has broken, or you have been bereaved. If you are shy or have a problem saying No when you need to, join a voluntary organization. Many of these have befriending schemes. The Samaritans is a well-known example, but there are hundreds of others. In the UK most towns have a voluntary services organizer who can direct you to the most appropriate one.

Donating

This could be giving money to a charity whose cause is related to your hurt. It could also be giving away material goods. A couple of examples might be giving a lost relative's clothes or possessions to a charity shop, or your copy of a book on recovering from divorce to a friend whose husband has just deserted her. You might also donate goods that you have made and that will be appreciated by others who are struggling with the hurtful problem that you had (e.g. making a cake for a bereaved family or helping to build a shelter for someone who has been made homeless by 'an act of God' similar to one that took your home away).

Fundraising

Don't be overawed by the new professionals and celebrities who raise millions. Remember this is still a healing step for you. So shaking a charity tin in a shopping centre or going on a short fundraising walk in aid of the issue that is important to you can be very effective Channelling. I have recently decided that whenever I am asked to do a free talk, I will now always ask for a donation (however tiny) to the school in Uganda we are building in the name of our daughter, Laura. This is a way I can easily fundraise a little without adding more pressure to my already busy schedule. Her sister, who is even busier than I am, found another way to do this. She recently used her fitness regime of running to complete the London Marathon in aid of Build Africa (http:// www.build-africa.org), the charity that is building the school in Africa in her sister's name.

Voluntary Work

For those of you who have some spare time, you could Channel by doing something practical to help a charity or organization that does good work, but has a limited budget and cannot afford more paid staff. You could, for example, join a group delivering first aid at work because your friend had an industrial accident; organizing Christmas presents for the underprivileged, because you had so few yourself; delivering meals-on-wheels, because they kept your grandfather alive for so many years; running play or visiting schemes for children in hospitals, because you remember feeling so isolated and scared as child with TB, or supplying new suits for job-seekers as you recall how despairing you felt when you were out of work for so long. But you could also use, like the UK's Terry Waite who was held hostage by Islamist extremists in Beirut for almost five years, some of your learning from your experience in your voluntary work. He said that being a hostage for that long taught him how to be patient. He explained that the charitable projects he supports, including the World Wildlife Fund, are mainly long-term, so this is a quality that is really appreciated and needed.

Paid Work

You don't have to become a psychotherapist or writer like me! Depending on the kind of experience you had, you could, for example become a:

- School crossing supervisor to stop children being hurt;

- Driving instructor to ensure people drive safely;

- Nurse or pharmacist to make sure medicines are more securely administered;

- Teacher to ensure every child has a chance to achieve their potential;

- Politician to make fairer policies;

- Building inspector to ensure buildings are safer;

- Vet's assistant to give more compassionate comfort to owners of sick and dying pets;

- Trade union official or employee relations advisor to help create fairer grievance procedures;

- A foster parent to give an orphan a chance of family life.

The possibilities for paid Channelling, if you are seeking a soul-satisfying as well as healing job, are endless.

Education

As your Perspective exercise should have revealed, your hurt has taught you something. Now you can find a way to pass on this learning either directly or indirectly. This could be informally to your children or friends and colleagues, or you could offer your wisdom and/or skill to an organization. For example, several people I know who have experienced breakdowns from burn-out or post-traumatic stress disorder have become stress-management teachers; another began to teach meditation and yet another joined a disaster response committee as an advisor.

You may also be able to benefit others by sharing your wisdom from the experience of even a minor hurt. A few months ago my husband was on an escalator in the London underground when two people appeared to block his way. He thought they hadn't heard or understood his polite request to pass them. It was only after a long, slow descent that, at the bottom of the escalator, one of these people turned round and he saw the words printed in large lettering on his sweatshirt, *Anti-Semite – and proud of it*, that he felt this had been a deliberately aggressive and racist act. When he arrived home, he was extremely upset, but thought that the incident would be considered too trivial to report. But after talking it through with me further, then Expressing his feelings and having some Comfort, he decided to report the incident to the police, even knowing that it was highly unlikely they could do anything. He thought that the information about this new kind of anti-Semitic activity might be useful to them. They were extremely grateful to him and, as it turns out, may now be able to use this information to pursue a prosecution.

Mentoring

This could be an ideal Channelling scheme for you if you experienced a hurt on your way up the career ladder. Maybe because of your personality, disability, race, gender or lack of access to formal education you experienced some injustice and would like to make it easier for other young people to break through such unfair barriers.

Erecting a Useful or Aesthetically Enhancing Memorial or Symbol

Popular ways of Channelling after a bereavement are to make or provide a garden bench, a tree or even a whole garden. We planted an oak tree for my father on one of his favourite spots and I planted cowslips, a friend's favourite flowers, in her memory. Similarly, you could create or commission a painting or sculpture or other work of art and place it somewhere relevant such as in a hospice or women's refuge.

Creative Writing

Tolkein, the famous author of *The Lord of the Rings* trilogy, had some traumatic First World War experiences in his early youth. He started writing while recovering from war wounds and is reported to have said that that is why his books are about the redemptive power of individual action. He wanted to give hope.

But you don't have to be a brilliant creative novelist. Siegfried Sassoon, another victim of the same war, wrote poetry that helped him and, later, millions of others. You mustn't worry too much about producing perfect or publishable writing. You could be just as healed, for example, by writing stories with a message for your grandchildren, staff at work, your local community newspaper, a club or charity newsletter or an internet friendship network. Most adult education establishments now run creative writing courses. Students on these are mostly writing from their life experiences. I have known many people use such groups for this purpose and they have found it a very supportive way to start this kind of writing project.

Devastated at the loss of his daughter in a senseless accident, Reg Thompson began writing letters to her about how the family was coping. His letters were then published in a moving book and serialized on the radio. When I heard them, I felt comforted and uplifted by his sharing, even though it brought back some tears. I am sure that many other bereaved parents must have felt similarly.

One of my readers recently wrote to me about a company that specializes in publishing writing done by people who have suffered mentally and emotionally, and want to share their experiences in order to help others. This reader, Julia Hope, has herself been published by them. Here is an extract of the letter that she wrote to me:

> *'I have written my story and it has been published as an e-book on Chipmunkapublishing.com. My story is called "Behind the dark clouds there is sunshine". It is inspirational and an honest account of how I suffered. But it is not all doom and gloom. It also tells of how I have completely turned things around now, and put my bad experience into good use by helping others. I wrote my story with the aim of helping others – it lets people know that there is light at the end of the tunnel. I very much want to help other sufferers. Please could you help me to do this?'*

Julia has had many emotional hurts and painful physical trials to contend with. I was moved by her efforts to help others now that she has herself recovered.

If your own writing skills are not up to the task, you can still use this powerful method of Channelling by asking others to write on your behalf. I asked the poet Wendy Cope, an admired idol of Laura's, to write a commemorative poem for her. Although we had only recently met, she very kindly agreed to do this. We used this beautifully written and moving poem on our fund-raising literature for the Foundation. It has since served the healing purpose by providing me with Comfort on many occasions when my grief has resurfaced in a painful way. A few lines of it are engraved on the back of the bench we installed for walkers on the path near where she was killed, so I hope they may give some Comfort to others who have suffered a premature bereavement.

Another creative writing option might be to contact your local amateur dramatic society. If you have a strong story with a powerful and helpful message, they might use a writer or improvisation to create a play.

Another alternative is to have your story creatively ghost-written by a professional author. Have a look on the internet or in reference books for companies or individuals that can help. The Society of Authors and the *Writers' and Artists' Yearbook* are good places to start. You'd be surprised by how many autobiographical works are produced in this way. In the current publishing climate, stories of people overcoming setbacks and tragedies are potentially big business. So, unusually in the field of creative writing, you may even make some money from the project for either yourself or a chosen charity.

Playing or Creating Music

In his later life, the death of the composer Gustav Mahler's elder daughter, Mariza, along with the trauma of parting from the Royal Viennese Opera and the early diagnosis of heart disease were almost unbearable for him. However, he threw himself into composing 'Das Lied von der Erde'. This work is now considered a masterpiece and people use it continually as solace from grief because it ends in acceptance and transformation.

If you are musically talented yourself you could, like Beth Nielsen Chapman, play or create your own music. After her husband was diagnosed with a rare form of lymphoma her music was put on hold. It was not until after his death that she started to write some of her most famous work. In an interview with the *Sunday Times* in 2005, she said:

In my life, music has often been an expression of the healing process. There were times in the first year after my husband's death that I was so busy looking after my son, I just didn't have time to cry. In the midst of all that bottled-up emotion I was writing the songs for 'Sand and Water' and I guess that served as my way of letting out that emotion.

Planting and Growing

Monty Don, a UK businessman, found that gardening had 'saved his life' when his jewellery business collapsed. After doing an interview on the radio about his experience, he received hundreds of letters from people saying how growing and tending a garden had helped in their recovery process, and he was invited to do many talks on the subject, including one to the Royal Horticultural Society. He has now written a book called *The Jewel Garden* which is about recovering from depression and disaster by creating a garden.

CHANNELLING IN A NUTSHELL

To use the learning from the experience of your hurt to help yourself or others, bear in mind that:

- Premature Channelling can be counter-productive.

- Perfection is not your goal.

- The progress of projects intended to help others needs to be monitored by objective outsiders.

- If you are aiming for an impressive 'halo', your Channelling may not be as effective for you or others.

7. Forgiveness

You have now reached the ultimate stage of the Strategy. The goal of Forgiveness is to be able to shake hands (physically or metaphorically) with the person or persons who perpetrated our hurt, and move forward into a new relationship with them which is completely free of resentment, grudges, prejudices and mistrust.

This kind of pure Forgiveness renders our wound not only healed but completely scarless. It is, however, very important to bear in mind that although genuine Forgiveness comes much more easily after you have done your essential healing it can still be extremely difficult to achieve. Sometimes it can take many years to reach this goal and sometimes, for various reasons that we shall discuss later, it will always be unattainable. So always bear in mind as you read this chapter that Forgiveness is a bonus stage rather than an essential one in the healing process. Rest assured that you can move on perfectly adequately from very many hurts without reaching this state of healing perfection. I have done so many times myself and seen very many others do so as well.

But if you think you may be able to achieve genuine Forgiveness it is well worth attempting to do so. Should you find that ultimately you cannot reach this goal, you will at least feel good about yourself for having tried. If, on the other hand, you are successful, not only will your own emotional well-being receive a boost but so will that of others. You are also likely to have a much stronger relationship with the people you have forgiven. This can be vitally important if the people are those whom you love or whom you need.

We now know that Forgiveness could also be one of the most

important keys to happiness. According to research, the route to personal bliss is not wearing designer shoes, driving an impressive car, living in a beautiful house on a tropical island or achieving international celebrity status. It is finding a way to live in a supportive community. This is so much easier to achieve if we are able to forgive each other for our imperfections, failures and wrongdoings.

On the macro front, another potential pay-off from Forgiveness is peace between warring factions and nations. The fledgling government of post-apartheid South Africa knew this. Their Truth and Reconciliation programme was a much admired attempt to achieve mutual forgiveness. The fact that they held this up as one of their key goals gave the community and the world around them an important injection of hope and motivation.

Similarly, mutual Forgiveness has also been an important factor in the rebuilding of peace in Northern Ireland after many years of bitter internal and external struggles. However suspicious some people may have felt about the genuineness of some of the handshakes that were displayed in the media, the fact that the opposing parties were seen to be working so hard to achieve Forgiveness must have been a crucial factor in maintaining peace.

Finally, many people also believe that Forgiveness is not just beneficial in this world but that it will also bring benefits in a possible next one as well. Many gods are hailed as great examples of Forgiveness and most religious preaching that I have heard encourages or commands people who have been hurt or wronged to forgive.

But, in spite of all these tempting benefits and the positive qualities of Forgiveness, it is still, in my opinion, not an essential component for emotional healing. In this respect, I would appear to be in disagreement with many other therapists and writers on this subject. In much of the literature, Forgiveness is often claimed to be the most important route to emotional recovery. For example, a quick Google search on Forgiveness and Emotional Healing reveals well over one million references. The following extracts are typical of the claims that are made in relation to Forgiveness.

Typical Comments on Forgiveness Found during a Recent Five-Minute Internet Search

- Forgiveness is truly the vital key to unlocking one's own bridges to healing and is a necessary connecting link to inner peace and wholeness.

- Forgiveness is the most radical form of healing.

- A growing number of therapists believe that Forgiveness is of crucial importance in helping people break away from patterns of resentment and revenge.

- Forgiveness is the key that can unshackle us from a past that will not rest in the grave of things over and done with. As long as our minds are captive to the memory of having been wronged, they are not free to wish for reconciliation with the one who wronged us.

- Traditionally the province of spiritual teachers, Forgiveness is being recognized as a powerful force in healing depression, anger, stress and physical illness.

- Recent studies have shown that practising Forgiveness can have a positive effect on our health.

This kind of unqualified 'preaching' about the fundamental importance of Forgiveness is not helpful to everyone who is attempting to recover from hurt. Indeed, it has the potential to be counter-productive. To those for whom Forgiveness is neither an option nor an insurmountable challenge, it can be demotivating. Many people suffering with emotional hurt who come to me for help are also weighed down with an unnecessary additional problem. They commonly feel guilty or inadequate because they cannot forgive.

WHY FORGIVENESS IS SOMETIMES IMPOSSIBLE TO ACHIEVE

Although it is fashionable in some therapeutic circles to think that we individuals are always responsible for our own luck, I believe that **freak accidents** do occur. Some hurts are caused by a number of random causative factors all merging together in an unpredictable way. The most obvious examples of this are of course natural disasters. Individual human error or other irresponsible factors such as global warming cannot be blamed for all of these disasters which leave so much emotional pain in their wake.

Similarly, Forgiveness is not an option if there just **isn't enough available evidence** for us to make an acceptable judgement about who or what was responsible. I can't Forgive the woman who disappeared from my daughter Laura's side after her fatal accident on a deserted country road at night even if I wanted to do so. I don't know who she was and there was not enough evidence to prove that she was indeed responsible. If Forgiveness is essential to healing, I guess I am a lost cause.

Sometimes people encounter the opposite problem. There is too much evidence and **an overwhelming number of people to forgive**. Just take a look at some of the causative factors that were going around in the head of Denise, a client of mine. Denise was in a state of high anxiety and rock-bottom self-esteem when she came to see me. She was kicking herself for not being able to forgive her husband who had been two-timing her. In our initial discussion she revealed that her husband:

- Had inherited a genetic tendency towards hypomania which made him more prone to recklessness than most people;

- Had a father who was a role model of infidelity;

- Came from a society where this behaviour was condoned rather than despised;

- Had low self-esteem caused by facial disfigurement gained from participating in justified strike action against an earlier employer;

- Had been expertly seduced by a woman who was known to be a 'gold-digger'. This woman, it emerged, had originated from an extremely poor society and had been sexually abused at four years old by her father and then sold as a sex slave at the age of twelve. She had freed herself by secretly studying and running away to find a job, but was sacked when an anomaly in her CV was spotted. She had 'picked up' my client's husband, who was a senior colleague, that same evening in a bar.

On top of all of these external factors, Denise talked about many other possible causes that were inside her psychological make-up as well. She felt she *should* be Forgiving, but was overwhelmed and confused. You can imagine what a relief it was to her to hear about this strategy. She realized that she had to accept that she might never know how much her husband was to blame, but that for the sake of her own emotional health and self-respect, this didn't matter. She actually didn't need to Forgive him in order to be able to move on.

As it happens, Denise's husband's attitude would not have made Forgiveness an option for her. He was passing the buck of responsibility rather than showing contrition or remorse. For our healing purposes, **Forgiveness is dependent on us truly believing that the perpetrator is genuinely sorry for what they have done or, indeed, would be truly contrite if they realized that their action or inaction had hurt us**.

Around the time of former US President Bill Clinton's scandal with Monica Lewinsky, there was a good deal of debate on the rights and wrongs of 'standing by your man'. As a therapist, the crucial issue for me was whether or not Hilary Clinton believed her husband's apology was genuine. My guess is that she did and was therefore able to forgive him. The super-healing and subsequent emotional resilience that she derived from doing so would certainly have stood her in good stead in the long-haul political challenge to become President she then set for herself.

But even if Denise's husband had appeared to be genuinely sorry, her **own code of morality** may have prevented her from Forgiving him. I believe that after listening to all sides of the story as we do in Perspective, we still have a right to make our own judgement about whether the 'sin' that has been committed is, according to our own ethical standards, forgivable. Denise's personal moral code may have differed from that of Hilary Clinton.

My own position on this question is that I believe the kind of serious hurts that have been perpetrated wilfully on vulnerable people and children are unforgivable. But I know that this is a personal moral view that many people disagree with.

If you do decide not to proceed with this step, there is still a chance that you could be hurt again. As long as Forgiveness remains highly esteemed and regarded as so fundamental to emotional healing by so many people, this will be the case. As a non-forgiver you run the risk of losing the respect of at least some people. You may be openly criticized for being unmerciful, judgemental or arrogant.

Non-forgivers, especially those who like Denise have had a struggle with their conscience, are also likely to suffer from guilt. This emotion can eat away at self-esteem and make us both feel and appear wimpish and highly attractive to predators and persecutors.

But these risks you take when you decide not to Forgive are, in my opinion, far less dangerous than those you could take by declaring your Forgiveness of certain perpetrators of hurt before you are truly ready, able or willing to do so.

THE DANGERS OF PREMATURE OR PHONY FORGIVENESS

Here are a few examples of the negative consequences of trying to Forgive before you are fully healed. Although some of these outcomes may sound extreme, the patterns of behaviour are all too common and you may well have encountered some of them:

- The pardoning partner who limps from one heartbreak to the next with the result that their self-esteem and sense of optimism are gradually eroded;

- The alcoholic who continually drowns his sorrows in order to be able to Forgive the hyper-critical attitude of the woman he loves;

- The martyr mother who is ever-forgiving of her children's selfishness and ends up deserted and lonely;

- The victim who forgives the bullies in an effort to impress them and ends up taking the blame for their misdemeanours;

- The son who continually forgave his dad's bullying, but then bullied his younger brother;

- The mother who forgives her husband's abuse of her child and is rejected and hated by her child when he or she reaches adulthood;

- The overly 'nice' boss who is given the push because his team didn't 'pull their weight' and missed their targets time and time again;

- The unassertive salesperson who forgave his pushy but charming colleague when she 'stole' clients from his patch and so continually earned less money;

- The battered wife who forgave just one too many times;

- The easy-touch father whose adult son doesn't work and shows no respect for him or his values.

As you are reading this book, I am aware that there is just a chance that you too might be someone who has a tendency to Forgive too easily or too quickly. If this is so, hopefully your problem has not caused you quite as much extra hurt as happened in the examples above. Perhaps your Forgiving habits are not that well entrenched and what I have already said could be enough to help you. I hope that it will at least make you think twice before knee-jerking into Forgiveness mode.

But sometimes just a warning about the pitfalls of a bad habit isn't enough. You may need to do some extra personal development work to gain control of your auto-response. You will need to tackle the problem at its root. Here are some examples of what you can do:

Root Cause	Recuperative Action
An over-developed need to please and be seen as nice	Strengthen your self-esteem and learn assertiveness techniques.
Fear of anger and rocking the boat	Learn anger management and strengthen your self-confidence.
Religious or other moral education	Review and check out your beliefs. Find out about other types of moral standpoints on the subject of forgiveness. Ask someone to test the strength of your principles by playing Devil's Advocate with you.

PRACTISING FORGIVENESS

Enough said on the problems at this stage. Let's move on to looking at how we can, if we are ready and truly willing, reap the positive benefits of Forgiveness. Here are some guidelines that I hope you will find encouraging and useful.

Be Proactive

How often have you heard (or uttered?) remarks like these?

1. 'I'm not speaking to him again until he says sorry.'
2. 'It's not up to me to make the first move – she was in the wrong.'
3. 'They don't care. It doesn't mean anything to them if they have to sack 100 staff. Companies are only interested in balance sheets and once they know you are leaving they couldn't care a damn.'
4. 'She's just a typical teenager. There's no point – they only think of themselves and their friends.'

In my job I hear similar comments much too often for my liking. This kind of talk (however understandable) is a sign that someone has given up their personal power – and, to make matters worse, they have delegated that power to the perpetrator of their hurt! Crazy? Yes, of course, but don't we all sometimes say and do crazy, self-sabotaging things when we have been emotionally hurt?

This kind of talk is also a sign that these people are not yet fully healed. If they were, their talk should be different at this stage. They would be planning to be proactive and, instead, be saying:

1. 'I am going to tell him that the reason I haven't been speaking to him for so many years is that he hurt me

very badly. I am hoping that he will then realize what
he did and apologize. If he doesn't, then I will
continue not to have any contact.'

2. 'It would have been nice if she had come up to me
    and apologized without me having to say anything.
    But she didn't. I could give her the benefit of the
    doubt and talk to her. Perhaps she didn't realize how
    hurtful she was and has hardly given the incident a
    thought since. Perhaps when she knows how long it
    has taken for me to get over this she will apologize.'

3. 'Balance sheets may be what companies are about at
    the bottom line, but a disregard for the feelings of
    staff that they make redundant could affect profit
    margins. People who are treated with disrespect will
    often bad-mouth the people who disrespected them.
    They can and do do this at any time and there is
    always a chance that they might meet a potentially
    valuable new recruit, or even the CEO of one of
    their major clients in a queue at the airport or in the
    supermarket! Perhaps if I tell them that this is what
    I have been tempted to do on several occasions, they
    will apologize and change their company policy.
    After all, they are not all rats in that company; there
    are many caring and sensitive people.'

4. 'Teenagers are indeed often self-obsessed. That is
    natural. But this is also an important time for them to
    learn about the consequences of their behaviour.
    I could choose a quiet moment to tell her how much
    she hurt me and say that I would feel a good deal
    better if she could just tell me that she was sorry.'

Before dismissing Forgiveness as an option, you can at least try
to elicit the apology you crave. If you don't get it, you will still
feel better because you defended yourself and made your feelings
heard.

188 THE EMOTIONAL HEALING STRATEGY

Assess the Risks

There are of course some perpetrators who will never apologize and should never be approached again unless it is absolutely necessary. This is certainly true of the egocentric, unashamed people who have a record of being persistently violent, emotionally manipulative or coldly calculating. It is also true of people who may suffer from a mental or psychological disorder that means they do not have full control over their actions.

So it is important that you do a risk assessment before you attempt to get an apology. It is often useful to talk this through with someone else who can view the risk more objectively. You'd be surprised by how many highly intelligent people I have met who have been hurt by the above kinds of people and, after years and years of evidence to the contrary and several severe hurts, still believe that they, and often they alone, can transform them. As I struggled for so many years with this problem myself, I know how important it is to have help with my own risk assessments when I want to reconnect with perpetrators of hurt. Depending on the experience you have had you will need to consider various factors. If you do the following exercise it will help you see what these are and fix them more firmly in your mind.

Instant Exercise: Assessing the Risks of Seeking an Apology

Select an emotional hurt for which you have not, as yet, forgiven the perpetrator, and ask yourself the following questions. If you cannot think of a real hurt, imagine one that you could possibly get some time from someone you know.

Tick the box if your answer is or would be 'Yes':

- ☐ Do you think the perpetrator has sufficient self-awareness to be able to understand what he or she has done?
- ☐ Have they shown by their past behaviour that they can admit their faults?
- ☐ Is your own current level of emotional resilience good enough to withstand rejection or another hurt?

3 ticks = low risk; 2 ticks = medium risk; 1 or 0 ticks = high risk

Assess What You Have to Gain

The pay-offs for the forgivers are arguably as great as they are for the forgiven. Forgiving boosts our self-esteem, our sense of personal power and our reservoirs of optimism. But it can also open the door to the possibility of a much closer and more satisfying relationship with the person or people whom we have forgiven.

Many of my clients either have a fundamental lack of self-esteem and/or have developed a self-sabotaging lifestyle and, to make matters worse, blame themselves totally for their problems. Part of my job is to help them do a reality check on who, or what, might have some share of the responsibility for their psychological make-up and long-term behavioural habits. Not surprisingly, at least one aspect of their parenting is found to be amongst the root causes. Most people are highly motivated to Forgive their parents, but sometimes this can prove to be quite a challenge. So I am often still supporting and encouraging my clients through this stage.

When Forgiveness is achieved, the pay-offs can be life changing for both parties. A few weeks ago a client from many years back rang me. She wanted to tell me that her mother had died and to thank me for all the healing work we had done together on their relationship. It had enabled her to Forgive her mother and rebuild a close relationship with her. She explained that she was particularly appreciative now because she could see that her sister, who had not done this, was now full of regrets and so her grief was much harder to bear.

Visualize a Good Outcome

Just as the sports stars do, visualize a scene in your mind of being successful and shaking hands with the other person or getting another kind of good outcome. This will help you to sound positive and increase your chance of getting what you want. Putting yourself into a positive mood should also help you to cope with rejection if that is the result, because you are more likely to come up with good ideas to help you recover.

Plan a Reward for Yourself, Whatever the Outcome

If you plan an enticing reward for yourself, whatever the result, it will help reduce your anxiety. You would deserve one for trying anyway.

Prepare a Script Before You Speak

As I have suggested in earlier chapters, it always pays to prepare a script that you can rehearse before entering an anxiety-provoking scenario. This will give you a chance to prepare assertive answers for any irrelevant excuses they may bring up. Often these are not true anyway, so don't get sidetracked by them. Just repeat your central message until the excuses stop and, hopefully, the apology arrives.

For example, repeating variations on the responses like those in the examples below would work. Note that they don't pick up on the excuses. To do so would be side-tracking and might possibly start an argument which could hurt you again.

Perpetrator: 'I was only thinking of your own welfare.'

Assertive response: 'But the point is that I was very hurt by your behaviour, and it would make a big difference to me if you could just say you are sorry.'

Perpetrator: 'The hospital usually maintains excellent standards of cleanliness. We have been struggling this year to keep these up with the cutbacks and have had no choice but to reduce staff ratios on the ward.'

Assertive response: 'The fact remains that, as the enquiry concluded, it was a failure to comply with the routine hygiene rules that caused my mother's fatal infection. Her premature death has been devastating for me and my family. We would now appreciate a formal apology from the Hospital Trust.'

Practise Your Body Language

Don't forget to match your words with confident body language: direct eye-contact; strong voice using even tone; upright relaxed posture and no fidgeting.

Write, if You Can't Speak

This is not a cop-out. You have been hurt and deserve to make it easy on yourself. To make an impact, write a typed letter to an authority or person you don't know and send a well-chosen card to someone you know well. Don't be tempted to send an email for ease and speed.

Be Alert For Signs of Phony Remorse

Look for signs which might indicate that the perpetrator is not really sorry. The classic body signals of lying can be a give-away. If you see a few of these, back off before you get hurt and have that reward fast!

- Beady eyes (constricted pupils);
- Shifting gaze;
- Biting lip;
- Covering mouth;
- Shifting from one foot to other;
- Fingers tugging ear.

Renegotiate or Request the Change You Want Before Shaking Hands

Once you have your apology, it may be appropriate to negotiate and agree 'rules' to try to ensure that you or someone else does not get hurt again. When you do, ensure that you spell out your expectations clearly, and the consequences if these are not met.

'Can we agree that in future you will check your facts before publicly criticizing me again? If this were to happen again, it would be the end of our friendship forever.'

'Can we be assured that the hygiene standards will now be upgraded and regularly checked? If you cannot give us that assurance, we will have to approach the Ministry of Health, or the media if they fail to respond.'

Use Your Imagination if the Perpetrator is Not Available or is Dead

You can still achieve Forgiveness if you truly believe that, if the perpetrator was able to hear how they have hurt you, they would be sorry. When I am working with a client we may sometimes test this out by doing a role play in which the hurt person plays the perpetrator. This is a technique we commonly use for childhood hurts where we suspect that the parent was basically well-meaning.

Another similar exercise is to write a letter, as the perpetrator, in response to your explanation of the hurt and request for an apology.

Talking to people who knew the person better than you did might also help you to make a judgement that may enable you to Forgive.

If you do decide to Forgive, you can use drama to enact an imaginary Forgiveness scenario or you could perform a symbolic ritual such as putting flowers on their grave or in front of their photo.

FORGIVENESS IN A NUTSHELL

To forgive the person or persons who were responsible for hurting you, and move forward into a new relationship with them which is completely free of resentment, grudges, prejudices and mistrust, bear in mind that:

- It is not possible to achieve Forgiveness in relation to every hurt known to mankind.

- Attempts to achieve Forgiveness can be risky.

- You have a right to make your own judgement about whether or not you even want to take the Forgiveness step.

- Phony Forgiveness is not healing.

- For Forgiveness to be healing the perpetrator must be truly sorry, or you must believe they would be if they realized how hurt you had been.

- You can be proactive and ask for an apology if one has not been given.

- New expectations or rules for the relationship may need to be agreed.

Post-Healing

8. Living with the Enduring Hurt

As the anniversary of a disaster or traumatic event approaches, many survivors report a return of restlessness and fear. Psychological literature calls it the anniversary reaction and defines it as an individual's response to unresolved grief resulting from significant losses. The anniversary reaction can involve several days or even weeks of anxiety, anger, nightmares, flashbacks, depression or fear.

On a more positive note, the anniversary of a disaster or traumatic event also can provide an opportunity for emotional healing.

USA Department of Mental Health

Perhaps you have an emotional hurt that has cut so deep that you fear it can never be completely healed. You may be right. The reality is that a small minority of wounds, even after the healing process that I have described is completed, will always remain fragile. There is a danger of them being reopened from time to time. If this happens, it may be enough just to do a quick repeat of the first few stages of the strategy. Occasionally, however, some can be so severe that you may have to learn to live with a residual amount of inner emotional pain for many years or forever.

It is very difficult to say which kind of wound is likely to come into either of these categories for you. As we have already seen, our individual reaction to different emotional hurts varies tremendously, because so many factors affect the level of pain we can experience.

A very small minority of these kinds of hurt are the severely traumatic ones that may have, for example, arisen from major disasters, serious crimes or wars. These could have been so psychologically destructive that they are not amenable to any form of self-help maintenance and may require long-term professional help. But we can usually do something ourselves to make living with more common serious hurts a little easier. Some examples of this type are:

- The death of someone who was deeply loved and played a major role in our life (such as a parent, partner or best friend);

- The break-up of a relationship in which there had been a very deep level of trust or intimacy over an extensive period of time (Those made during the brain's still-forming years of adolescence or during a traumatic period such as wartime or after a major loss are most likely to endure.)

- Violent physical or sexual abuse;

- The death of a child or a parent or parent figure;

- The causing of deliberate irreparable emotional hurt to one or more of our children;

- The permanent loss of contact (or meaningful contact) with a child;

- A persistent deprivation in childhood of a basic psychological need (such as the need to be loved unconditionally, feel secure and trust others);

- The permanent loss of or severe damage to part of our body;

- The permanent deprivation or impairment of a physical or mental function.

Have you experienced any of the above? If so, you will know why I am writing this chapter. Although I haven't personally experienced all of the above, I have had to learn to live with the majority. The rest I have encountered a fair number of times in my professional work.

As you must know already, people's capacity to live with these enduring kinds of hurts varies enormously. Some people become cynical, bitter, chronically sad, persistently fearful, seriously addicted or reclusive. Others appear to be able to maintain their optimism and live relatively happy and successful lives in spite of their residual sadness, anxiety or disappointments. Of course, some of these differences can be accounted for by factors that we have already discussed such as personality make-up, environment or even luck. But I am convinced that what people do to manage their enduring hurt is also an important differentiating factor.

> Someone once told me that having a dead loved one is like living next to a dangerous deep river. It's always there, you can fall into it, and suffer, you can walk alongside it, and look into it, and feel its danger and its depth, you can admire it for its own identity, its own being. You'd much rather it wasn't there and that you could walk somewhere safe and peaceful, but you can't. You've got to go on walking by the side of it.
>
> Michael Rosen

When Laura died, I knew (like most bereaved parents do) that I would be grieving for her forever. Interestingly for me, this was the first time in my life that I also realized that this was an emotional wound that *I didn't want* to recover from completely. I felt instinctively that if I stopped feeling sad and occasionally heartbroken about this loss, I would lose out in other ways as well. At the time it was impossible to put into words what I meant by this, but I now know. If I 'recovered' so well that I no longer felt any resurgence of grief, I would also lose some positive aspects of the experience which I have highlighted on the next page.

I believe that if I was completely cured of the hurt of Laura's death, I would lose:

- **A valuable part of me that was created by my experience** of being a mum to Laura. I sometimes need to be reminded of that part of me. For example, Laura often awakened the fun-loving and spontaneous side of me. When I am feeling her loss, I often think of this and it helps me reconnect with that part of me, which is a great stress reliever and makes life much more worth living.

- **The motivating energy** which I feel I need to continue to Channel my hurt into constructive use. This has indeed been useful when I have writer's block or have a backlog of uninviting administration to do in relation to my therapeutic or charity work.

- **The heightened sensitivity** to the problems that the rest of the family still has as a result of Laura's tragic death.

- **The ongoing comforting connection** which I still have with Laura. Although I do not have a belief in an afterlife, I feel that she is 'here' in some respect. She still plays an influential role in my life. I often hear myself saying things like: 'Laura would have laughed about this,' or 'Laura would have said, "Don't be so silly, go for it and enjoy it."' When I speak in this way, it is as though Laura is truly watching what is going on. (This is a common hallucinatory symptom, and it could be argued that it is a form of denial. If it is, I don't believe it is the destructive kind that we discussed in the Introduction to the Emotional Healing Strategy, which sabotages healing. Its effect is undoubtedly positive rather than negative.)

So I believe I have some very good reasons for *wanting* to keep some of the sadness and anger inside me as long as I live. But I am also aware that carrying around this inner wound with me is a major responsibility. It has to be nursed well. It has to be protected as much as possible and when it's knocked by a memory or another new experience of grief, I must ensure that it is 'treated'. If I neglect it I know that there is a danger that it could become septic and sour my mind and my life.

> All we want to do is forget. Not forget *her*, as if we could, as if we would want to, but forget *it*. But we can't . . . to recover would, for him, be the greatest betrayal.
>
> Margaret Forster, *Over*

Instant Exercise

Think of a past hurt from which you still have some residual painful feelings.

● Note down the positive benefits that having occasional emotional reminders of this hurt has brought or could bring. As in my examples above, the benefits might include ones for other people as well as yourself.

How to Manage Your Enduring Hurt

In doing the above exercise you have already taken two very important steps in the management of your hurt. First, you have acknowledged that the hurt is still there (albeit in a very mild form). Secondly, you have appreciated that there are some positive benefits to having it still present within you. However, these steps may not be enough to help you to stay in good-enough control. If this kind of inner pain is left unattended and pushed to the back of our minds, it can suddenly well up if it meets a reminder as it did for these people.

'I was in the queue at the bank, and someone about his age and black just pushed in ahead and I flipped. I've not even thought about it for ages. It was so embarrassing.' (A woman who had been raped eight years previously while on holiday in Africa)

'A group of us were out having a meal and I was really enjoying it. Then someone just started talking about how their mum was coming over to look after the kids and how excited they were about going off with her and I started to cry. I suppose I must have been missing Mum since having the baby more than I thought.' (A woman who lost her mum three years ago)

'I let Sonia deal mostly with the kids now. I once lost my cool with Adam and that did it.' (It emerged that this man recalled being consistently hit by his father as a child, often because his younger brother 'sneaked' on him. Adam, his youngest son, has the similar charming cheeky nature that his brother has.)

Such uninvited outbursts of emotion can be disconcerting, embarrassing, occasionally dangerous or simply inconvenient. They can also sabotage our efforts to move on in our life because we may start to avoid the situations where there is a risk that our hurt will surface. This can be severely limiting for us and it can sometimes be frustrating, or annoying, for other people. It can be particularly risky in certain work situations. In the immediate aftermath of a serious hurt, most colleagues and bosses are sympathetic and tolerant. But, in today's stressful workplaces, this tolerance tends to have a very short shelf-life. Even if people do not openly say, 'I think you should have got over that by now,' they may be inwardly irritated or even afraid of your 'frailty'. As a result, they may find excuses not to give you the pressure and responsibility that you need to have in order to progress with your career.

Misery is a communicable disease.

Martha Graham

It is not just in the workplace that we can miss out. If our feelings are not well enough under our control, they can also cause difficulties in our personal relationships. It's hard to be spontaneous while walking on eggshells around a sensitive someone. At the very least, this means that we may lose out on many moments of easy-going conversation; fun; light teasing and passion that nurtures intimacy. At worst, some people might avoid or reject us for being too hot to handle. Such people are not necessarily bad people (and therefore not worth knowing anyway); they may just feel out of their depth for a very good reason. Indeed, they could be just the kind of empathic people who could help you to live with your hurt.

I have found it helpful to consider living with an enduring hurt as an emotional disability. This may sound a little overdramatic, but I've found that it helps people to see that an ongoing emotional wound deserves both respect and care to ensure that it does not limit us unnecessarily. We may not, like people with physical disabilities, need special legislation, adapted walkways or financial grants, but we do need to make special allowances for our own emotional fragility. We also need actively to protect and care for our inner wound. If we do this, we can minimize the risk of unexpected 'flare-ups', and we will become more emotionally resilient to new knocks that could re-open our wound.

I believe that, while we may not need to demand direct help from others in the care of this kind of wound, we still have the right to expect their respect. This is particularly true when we are making an effort to manage our residual pain. It isn't helpful, for example, to be told or reminded that others have 'soldiered on' in spite of worse things happening to them, or that we are too 'touchy' for our own good. So remember it wasn't easy for them, and it won't be for you; but it is possible. If you should choose, for example, not to enter into certain discussions, visit some places or throw away memorabilia because you do not want to trigger more painful emotion than you can manage, others should respect your choice. But, of course, you must first be sure that you are doing everything in your power actively to manage and care for your hurt. Here are some suggestions that I hope will help you to do this.

HOW TO PROTECT AND CARE FOR YOUR ENDURING HURT

Make Casual References in Conversation

The biggest mistake most people make is trying to keep their enduring hurt too firmly fixed in the back of their mind. Instead it is better to make it a reasonably regular feature in conversation, but at your calling. You must choose when and where to bring up the subject. If you do this you will stay in control emotionally and the topic will not become a 'hidden skeleton' in a cupboard that you are terrified of opening, or having opened by anyone else.

Try referring to it casually and unemotionally in conversation while discussing another topic. Here are a few examples that I have used in relation to my loss of Laura:

- *'Thanks. It was interesting how after Laura died I started to gain more confidence in my own ability to choose colour schemes. Before that, because she was considered the artist in the family, we all naturally tended to defer to her opinion on creative matters.'* (A passing mention of a positive outcome of the hurt after being complimented on the new décor of our flat.)

- *'Yes, I have been to Cadiz. My daughter and I were there just after Laura died. But that was eleven years ago – it must have changed a good deal since then. What is it like now?'* (An incidental neutral reference to a place that still evokes emotionally charged memories.)

Prepare and Tell Your Story

At the end of the chapter on Perspective, I suggested that you prepare a very short story of your hurt. You can have this, or similar ones, prepared and ready to tell whenever you may need them. This could be when the subject comes up in the form of a question or comment from someone else. If you don't want to respond, you can use the assertiveness tips below. But a controlled response coming in a well-balanced way from both the heart and the head will not destabilize you emotionally. It might well also have some positive influence on the other person. So you would gain some bonus healing from the Channelling.

Here are some examples of prepared responses that have worked. I have highlighted the parts of the response that had already been scripted:

- **Comment:** 'What did you think of the sentence meted out by that new judge on that rapist the other day? It was a bit over-the-top, wasn't it?'
  Answer: 'I am pleased the judicial system is now taking this crime more seriously. **I was raped ten years ago when I was only sixteen years old. That man is now free, but I will never be completely free of the emotional hurt that he caused.** Because of my own experience I keep a keen eye on what is happening in this field. I believe that we still have a long way to go in this country with respect to dealing with rape. Recent research showed that at 5.3 per cent, our conviction rate is the lowest in Europe.'

- **Comment:** 'All parents want the best for their children.'
  Response: 'Unfortunately, that's not true in many families. **My mother was extremely jealous of me and whenever I had any kind of success in my**

work at school or with boyfriends, she would make a spiteful comment. She didn't attend my graduation because she had an important bridge party to go to. Although I now know that she was very insecure and bitter for good reasons, the memory of her negative attitude still hurts me and it has been a great struggle to overcome it. My story is not unusual. I heard similar ones and some that were much worse when I was going to my dramatherapy sessions.'

- **Comment:** 'I told him that in a couple of years he won't give her, and all her lies, a thought. He'll probably be happily married by then – don't you men forget more easily than women anyway?!'
  Response: 'Actually, his experience is very similar to one that I had around the same age. **My first wife had an affair with my best friend.** Although it was twenty years ago, I still feel my gut churning when I hear of something like that happening. A betrayal like that from someone you loved and trusted can be hard for anyone to forget. **Even being happily married to Jan for fifteen years hasn't cured me completely of the mistrust that I still have deep inside me.'**

. . . they bring Kath back to life, passing her to and fro between them . . . they are clear eyed; they do not remember with sentimentality.

Penelope Lively, *The Photograph*

Protect Yourself with Assertiveness

In the example above, the person asking the question in relation to rape sentences might be someone with whom you would prefer not to discuss such a sensitive subject. Alternatively, you might not feel in the mood to tell your story at a particular time or in that particular place. In any such situation, you could use a well-rehearsed assertive response to put up a 'no-go-area' barrier.

The classic self-protective assertiveness strategy called 'Fogging' would be very useful in this kind of situation. It stops any possible argument or discussion in its tracks by suggesting that there *might* be some truth in what the other person has said (even though inwardly you know that there is not): 'You could be right. Maybe it is not the right sentence.'

Fogging almost always has the effect of stone-walling the other person into silence or changing the subject. If you find this difficult to believe, ask a friend to try it out with you. If you take the role of the questioner you will soon find out that it works.

Alternatively, if you have enough confidence, a firmly delivered assertive statement such as, 'That is a topic I'd prefer not to discuss,' can do the same trick.

If the questioner moves on to ask, 'Why not?' you can (accompanied by a smile and direct eye contact) then reply, 'I'd rather not get into discussing my reasons for not doing so either!' If you want further guidance on how to use this technique, just watch politicians being interviewed!

Practise Emotional Control Techniques Regularly

However prepared you are, there may be the odd times when you are caught so off-guard by a comment or question that your emotion will well up. In these circumstances, it is important to get a calming technique into action as quickly as possible. This is why you need to be in the habit of using these techniques regularly.

Your brain's responses must be so well programmed that they can go into instant action. You may not have the chance to do one of the techniques suggested for Expression in full, but just doing some deep breathing and reminding yourself of the visual imagery, music, mantra or colours will be enough to calm your pulse and enable you to take control. In these kinds of circumstances, I recall an image that I use in my 'Imaginary Stroll' visualization. In emergency situations, in order to calm myself, I visualize a fountain in the garden where I take my imagined walk. I also keep a picture of this fountain at hand so I can look at it regularly. Doing this reinforces the association in my brain between the fountain and physical calm.

Regularly practising your calming techniques will also help to keep your everyday stress levels low. This is important because the calmer you are, in general, the less likely you are to respond to extra stress in panic mode.

Control Your Input of Unnecessary Hurtful Reminders

This is perhaps an obvious suggestion, but I include it because so many people I meet seem to need it pointed out. Obviously, it may be difficult, if not impossible, to rid yourself of all reminders. Indeed, you may not want to do that. But you can usually ensure that you are only regularly confronted with the number that you can deal with emotionally.

Let's look first at the kind of reasons that people commonly give for hanging on to unnecessary reminders:

- 'It would feel as though I was deserting him if I got rid of his clothes from the wardrobe.'

- 'People might think I didn't really didn't care that much if I took it down and put up a picture instead.'

- 'I can't stop going to the Rape Crisis meetings each
  week – it would feel as though I was letting them
  down . . . I know I have done my bit as I have been
  going for seven years.'

- 'I'm frightened that I might forget her altogether if I
  moved because sometimes I find it so difficult to just
  recall her face.'

- 'After what I went through as a result of my marriage
  break-up, I wanted to become a voluntary counsellor,
  but now I wonder if it is just too difficult for me to
  keep on being reminded. But I feel as though I owe
  it to them because they gave me so much training.'

What these people have in common is that they are putting up
with an emotional overload of pain unnecessarily. They are
allowing themselves to be constantly reminded of their hurt
because they have made false or impossible-to-check-out assumptions
about the views or needs of others.

The human mind can bear plenty of reality, but not too much
uninterrupted gloom.

Margaret Drabble

Where possible and appropriate, you can test out your assumptions
with the people you are concerned about. My experience
has shown me that when you do, they are almost always very
understanding. If, as in my first example, the person is no longer
with you, you have to use your knowledge of the person to help
you imagine what they would say if they could be asked. To help
one client to do this recently, I shared this personal story.

'When Laura died, I tried to continue living in the same house
and same town but after a year, I decided that I wanted to move
to a new location that had no memories of our life with her. This
wasn't because I wanted to forget her as I am sure by now

you appreciate, it was because I didn't want hurtful reminders surfacing so frequently. My husband didn't feel the need to do this in spite of his continuing deep grief, but he understood and respected my need to do so, so we moved.'

This sharing helped my client to realize that her husband would have done the same. She knew that her husband would not want her to suffer unnecessarily so she took his clothes to a charity shop. She really needed someone else to give their blessing to her doing so. You could ask a friend to do this for you.

This kind of choice about whether to face or not to face regular reminders also has to be confronted by people with other kinds of hurts. It is a common dilemma for people who have been passed over for promotion. Most of the people I know who have experienced this have chosen to leave their job – even though it was not the best career or personal move for them. They have said that they felt they did not want to cope with being continually reminded of what had happened. But in contrast, I have one friend who was (in most observers' eyes) unfairly demoted during a re-engineering of the management structure. To my surprise and to that of his colleagues, he chose to stay. I remember admiring his courage and emotional resilience. A few months ago, I talked to him about this decision. He told me that it was indeed extremely difficult to stay on. He had done so for his family's sake as they had only just settled in the area. He said that he knew he had the ability to manage his feelings at work, so he felt able to make that sacrifice. But, interestingly, he also said that the joy went out of his work. As Compensation, he put energy into preparing for early retirement in a dream location which he now enjoys. This helped him to see the demotion in Perspective. He did move on, but he says that the hurt of what happened is still there. Because of this, he now chooses to have as little contact as possible with the people in the company that he worked with for so many years.

This story about my friend's experience set against my own about my house move highlights the need for each person making their own decision about what level of discomfort they can or cannot cope with. But remember, before making your choice, to check your assumptions with others. If their needs are different, don't give in before explaining clearly what problems you are having. You can always negotiate.

Organize Regular Outlets for Safe Expression Followed by Some Comfort

This is perhaps the most important suggestion of all. It seems to help everyone who has enduring hurt.

Make sure that, every so often, you take yourself to a place where you can safely give some Expression to your inner feelings and then, later, have some Comfort. How you do this will vary with each hurt and the type of feelings associated with it.

In most cultures, if grief has been shared by a community, for example following a natural disaster, war or multiple murder, an annual communal memorial ritual will often be organized. In some countries such as Mexico, one day is set aside in the national calendar as a holiday when everyone has an opportunity to remourn any lost loved ones. However, in my experience, people do not always organize similar rituals for themselves for their own personal losses. This is such a pity as it is easy and so healing to do.

If you have lost a loved one, you could try giving yourself some memorial time at a quiet, secluded spot. This could be in the country or a town or simply in a room in your house where you can be assured of privacy and peace. You can provide your own comfort in the form of a treat to eat while you are there or just taking time to indulge in listening to some favourite music.

An alternative might be to go back to a place that has positive associations with the person you loved and recall the happy memories. This usually puts sadness into motion, but in an uplifting way. This is because it is a gentle, indirect way to remind yourself of the wise and comforting words of the poet Lord Tennyson:

... 'tis better to have loved and lost than never to have loved at all.

These personal rituals are especially important to do on or around difficult dates. Our family tries to programme into our diaries time to be together for at least a few hours on Laura's birthday and on the anniversary of her death. We used to visit the commemorative bench we installed by the roadside where she had her accident, but one year this simply didn't seem to be what we wanted to do. Perhaps we had just had enough of focussing on the tragedy and wanted to remember Laura in other ways. Now we go to a church wherever we happen to be. We light a candle and just think about her. I may weep a little, but most of the time I am recalling wonderful memories and pleasantly fantasizing about what she might be doing if she were alive today. We are not religious, but have found churches (of differing denominations) very welcoming and peaceful places in which to do this. If we cannot be together, we will all perform this little ritual in different countries so we still feel together. After going to the church we will take ourselves off for afternoon tea which has traditionally been our favourite family treat.

If your loss has been the result of a happening other than death, you can still arrange to give some time for Expression. For example, many people who are living with the residual pain of a major heartbreak would be considerably helped by giving themselves an outlet to release some feeling on significant days such as a wedding anniversary or Valentine's Day. You may feel that if you are now in another relationship, this shouldn't be necessary. But you can counter this feeling by remembering that doing something (discreetly of course) that is helping you towards better emotional health is likely to benefit your new relationship. You could, for example, just spend a few quiet moments looking at photos and recalling happy memories, then giving yourself a small Comfort treat. Or you could phone an understanding friend who will just listen to your outpourings and then help you to regain Perspective.

There is pleasure in calm remembrance of a past sorrow.
Marcus Tullius Cicero (106–43 BC)

If your hurt has been one where anger is the central feeling, it is equally important to do something which will regularly permit you to release any pent-up emotion. This could be done with the help of an appropriate self-help group or pressure group. For example, you could join a peaceful annual awareness-raising march or charity run. At these events you will meet like-minded people with whom you can tell your story, release your tension and give mutual Comfort, listen to others and gain perspective from seeing the Big Picture view of these experiences, while at the same time engaging in some constructive Channelling.

Reheal Promptly from Even the Smallest Resurgence of Old Hurts

Last night my husband told me that during the day he had been shocked to find himself experiencing one of these on the underground in London. He saw a man coming towards him who looked exactly like his primary school head teacher. He froze with fear. When he was later talking to me about the violent and unjust punishments he had received from this man (Exploring), his voice was shaky and his face screwed up (Expression). I was very moved by his pain and listened intently and, I hope, empathically (giving Comfort). We then went on to talk about the effects that this old hurt had had on him. How, for example, he used to allow himself to be bullied by certain bosses and clients at work. We acknowledged that it has taken years to overcome this 'victim' response to bullying behaviour. And he has since made sure that he works for companies where this behaviour rarely exists. We then laughed together as we acknowledged that it still can occasionally emerge when I get stressed and go into my bossy mode (Perspective).

Working through healing stages was done in just a few

moments. We were not consciously doing so. Acting in this way after a hurt has been re-ignited has now become a marital habit.

The perfectionists amongst you may have noticed that we missed out one stage – Compensation. Perhaps that was because we are both currently on diets! But seriously, this step wasn't strictly necessary. This was, after all, a re-emergence of an old hurt that has already been well compensated for throughout much of my husband's career.

So remember that if you do have an unexpected revival of an enduring hurt, don't dismiss it, deal with it. The most important stages of the strategy to go through on these occasions are the first three. With major hurts you may need some help to do this effectively. With more minor ones the Exploration can be done in your head, the Expression can be minimal and the Comfort can be self-administered. So no excuses about tight agendas and inappropriate locations are permissible!

Reflect Regularly on Your Emotional Health

Having given you all these suggestions for an emotional mainten- ance programme, I am enough of a realist to know that there will be times when it will go the way of many of my physical fitness programmes! One way of bringing yourself on track is to build in regular check-ups. How often you need to do this will depend partly on how many boxes you tick in the following checklist. If there is a large number, you might be advised to do monthly checks for a while. Later, you could just do them bi-annually or annually.

A good way to ensure you do your check-ups is to programme them into your diary. Taking short breaks which allow you to 'chill out' and do some self-reflection are ideal. If it is possible to go with someone who wants to do the same, you can encourage and help each other to keep to your resolutions on your return.

You can use this checklist to start the ball rolling. Your score will give you a *rough* assessment of the state of your emotional health. But the main purpose of the checklist is to help you focus on relevant issues and happenings.

EMOTIONAL HEALTH SPOT-CHECK

Tick the box if your answer is 'Yes' to any of the following questions:

☐ Have you found it harder or more upsetting than usual when you have listened to others' emotional problems?

☐ Have you been tearful for little reason?

☐ Have you found yourself playing safe or not bothering to argue back in conversations to keep order or to keep the peace?

☐ Have you been feeling anxious about anything that you would normally cope with well?

☐ Have you found yourself feeling resentful about something that has happened?

☐ Has anyone suggested that you have been oversensitive?

☐ Has anyone said you look upset when you didn't think you were?

☐ Have you been eating or drinking unhealthily?

☐ Have you often been waking up feeling tired rather than refreshed?

☐ Have any of your nervous habits (e.g. a tic or nail biting) become worse?

☐ Has your mind gone blank more than once or twice?

☐ Have you been more forgetful than usual?

☐ Have you had any aches, stomach upsets and pains that you know are usually caused or made worse by stress?

☐ Have you snapped at anyone?

☐ Have you found yourself feeling less tolerant about others' imperfections?

☐ Have you lost patience with frustrations (such as being on hold on the end of a phone or waiting for a bus or train that is late)?

☐ Have you had more trouble than usual getting off to sleep more than a few times?

☐ Have you been holding back on talking about your enduring hurts?

☐ Have you felt less loving than you normally do?

☐ Have you had less fun than you normally do or would like to have had?

☐ Have you found your mind wandering off into reminiscences or fantasy more than usual?

☐ Have you had more arguments than usual?

☐ Have you felt less at ease when on your own than you normally do?

☐ Have you been surprised by negative feelings?

☐ Have you been troubled by nightmares?

☐ Have you been more moody than usual?

☐ Have you felt less happy than you normally are?

☐ Have you felt less happy than you would like to be?

☐ Have you spent too little time with the people you love or care about?

☐ Have you been feeling pessimistic about your future or the future of the world?

☐ Have you been worrying persistently about anything?

☐ Have you been feeling more nostalgic of late?

☐ Have you been less productive than you normally are?

☐ Have you been less sociable than you usually are?

☐ Have you been feeling regretful?

☐ Have you been less caring to others than you normally are?

☐ Have you let your appearance go in any way?

☐ Have you been less generous on treats for yourself than you would like to have been?

☐ Have you been less tidy and organized than you normally are?

☐ Have you been finding it difficult to concentrate?

If you have ticked more than ten boxes, you may have some issues that could need attention. It is possible that recently there have been some unusual and temporary circumstances or happenings that have negatively affected you. If so, you may not need to worry too much if you are coping as well as can be expected. But as a double check, repeat the exercise in a month's time. If you then have as many or more ticks, you will know that your emotional health does need attention.

After doing this exercise, it may have become blindingly obvious what needs to be done. But it may not. Many of my clients who have presented with a fair number of these 'symptoms' didn't have a clue about what was going wrong in their lives. After talking to them a little more, it may become apparent that they have sunk into a mildly depressed state and their emotional responses have become generally flatter, so they are less sensitive to their feelings. To someone who has suffered a great deal with their feelings this may sound like a welcome relief, but it is not an emotionally healthy one.

If you think this is the case for you, you may also need some gentle confrontation from a friend (or a counsellor). It may be that you have been pushing a series of mini-hurts back inside without realizing that you have been doing so. Together, you can review in detail what has been happening, or not happening, in your life recently. You can also examine what has given you pleasure and what has not. When doing so, remember that we are likely to push negative feelings inside when:

- We are too busy to deal with them.

- We view a hurt as too minor to merit attention (especially in comparison to a major hurt we may still have inside).

- We are feeling happy and not wanting to 'spoil' the good feeling with a bad one.

- A hurt has triggered the same feeling as an old enduring one.

- We are feeling generally fragile or under too much stress.

- We have not wanted to upset or annoy the perpetrator of the hurt for a good reason.

- We are feeling physically under the weather and do not have enough energy to deal with hurt or discontent.

- Our self-esteem and/or self-confidence are at a low ebb.

After your reflection, it is very important to do a written action plan. Doing so will increase your chances of keeping your good intentions. Here is an example of a format you could use.

ACTION PLAN TO IMPROVE MY EMOTIONAL HEALTH

Possible Areas for Attention	Action
1. Balance of life	Speak to boss about reducing overtime. Stop looking at emails after 8pm.
2. Dealing with current hurt	Talk to Angie about that unfair criticism. Heal the disappointment about losing the flat.
3. Care of enduring hurts	Arrange to spend the 15th with sister.
4. Physical health	Go to bed earlier; take vitamins; stick to wholemeal bread and eat more fish, nuts and seeds; clear fridge of temptation.
5. Mindset	Ask Dave to tell me when I am moaning; watch news only once a day; spend more time with happy friends.
6. Self-esteem/Self-confidence	Have my hair restyled; focus on my strengths when worrying about a weakness; affirmations.

9. Helping Others to Heal

Hopefully, most of you will also want to apply your learning from this book not just to help yourself but to help others heal as well. Some of you will indeed have roles in your personal or work life which mean that you have some direct responsibility for helping others so I am including a few specific guidelines for anyone who cares for children or is in a leadership position. But first, here are some general pointers which I trust will be useful to anyone who wants to make the most of their compassion.

> The greatness of a community is most accurately measured by the compassionate actions of its members.
>
> Corretta Scott King

Don't Hesitate to Try

If your intentions are good there is very little chance of doing harm. These guidelines are only designed to help you refine your helping skills and protect you from suffering unnecessary hurt yourself. You already have the most crucial and valuable helping 'tool': your compassion. Nowadays I hear so many people say they are afraid of trying to help because they fear they may say or do the wrong thing and make matters worse. By just communicating your compassion and a genuine desire to help in whatever way you can, you will do a huge amount of good.

Play to Your Strengths

Hurt people can benefit from all manner of help. Practical help can be just as psychologically healing as counselling. It is a way of communicating that you care and can give protection and support which enables the hurt person to attend to their emotional needs. We often feel powerless, especially if someone is deeply distressed. If you do what you do best you will recover your confidence and be at your most effective.

So, first try to assess what they might need. Remember they may not be able to think what that is if they are emotionally upset. Then if you are:

- A good listener, listen (there are some tips from the professionals on pages 230–33 that might help you become even more of an expert);

- An articulate talker, help them find the words to express their feelings and needs;

- Someone who has experienced the same feelings, share your empathy;

- Great at making cakes, get baking;

- A good driver, be a chauffeur (upset people are not the best drivers);

- A dog lover, fetch the lead if one needs a walk;

- A good gardener, cut their lawn or pick them a beautiful bunch of fresh flowers;

- An organizer, get on the phone for them or help them make a to-do list (it is harder to think straight when you are upset);

- A natural leader, start rallying others into action if necessary;

- Highly assertive, stand up for them and their needs (they are likely to be less capable of fighting for themselves);

- A great networker, search your contact lists for sources of support;

- An expert on the computer, browse the internet for useful information or send emails for them.

Accept the Limitations of Your Energy

The big danger for helpers is burn-out. Helping emotionally hurt people drains both physical energy and emotional energy. 'Negative' emotions are contagious and the pressures of the crises can be exhausting. Don't become one of those notorious 'wounded healers' who stray out of their depth. When we are concerned about others, it is easy to neglect our own needs and health.

Stay aware of your true capabilities. One of the best ways to do this is to take notice of others' comments. If someone says, 'You look tired,' don't summon up a bright smile to convince them otherwise; take a rest. It they should spot that you have skipped a meal and offer to stand in for you, don't say you are not hungry; thank them and go to eat. If someone has spotted your swollen eyes or tense expression, don't claim you are fine; take time out to release your own emotional hurt.

Keep Your Focus on Being You in Your Normal Role

If you are a friend, be one, and don't attempt to be a detached or objective counsellor. The warmth of your subjectivity and your knowledge of the other person might be just what they need to help them Express their feelings or give them Comfort. If you are their boss, they may need a reality check on their performance more than they need your friendship. If you are their mum, they may need your cuddles and home cooking more than they need advice about the future of their career or relationship.

Accept that Your Ability to Help Those You Love May Be Limited

When our loved ones are distressed, it is natural that we will be too. It may at times be distracting or disturbing for the hurt person to see your pain. They may want to 'rescue' you rather than do what will help them recover best. One of the toughest life lessons I learned when my daughter Laura died was that until I healed myself, my own emotional healing skills were of little use to my other daughter or my husband. For a while I was even unable to give them support as mum or wife. Luckily, I was aware of this and dealt with my guilt by trying to ensure that they had quality support from others.

The same may be true when a minor hurt has occurred. Our emotional investment in our loved ones may still sometimes block us from giving them what they need. Even though we are well aware of the healing process, we may unconsciously be driven to do something to make them feel better such as distracting them with positive news we know they will welcome or giving them unsolicited advice, when they actually need to Explore their disappointment or frustration.

Remember that the very best thing we can do to help our hurting loved ones is to assure them through words and actions that we are at their side and will be so through thick and thin. We can only keep that promise if we stay strong and optimistic ourselves. This may mean letting others do what we would love to do, but cannot do as well as they can at this moment in time.

Stay Away From Those You Truly Don't Want to Help

There are no saints in this real world. We all have our prejudices. We are all capable of narrow-mindedness, discrimination and manipulation – especially when faced with people whom we don't like or those who exhibit types of behaviour that we abhor or that ignite our enduring hurts. Anyone who is in emotional pain is vulnerable, and however 'nice' we normally are, there is a very good chance that we will be tempted to take advantage of our relative power if we are in the position of helping them.

Even if you think you can control this temptation, any compassion you show is highly likely to come across as phony. Body language tells the truth. When they are fully healed, if you really want to help them, you can ask to engage in a rational conversation with them about your views and even offer some advice. The experience could be enlightening for them and for you too. But, like Forgiveness, this is an option and may not be a personal priority for you even if it may seem to be so for other people.

Encourage Self-Healing

Don't immediately launch into a massive lecture about the Emotional Healing Strategy (in the aftermath of hurt, they couldn't take it in anyway). But, as in this example below, you could gently encourage them into the first stage if they seem to be avoiding healing.

> **Hurt person:** 'Well, that's that. It's happened and I just have to get on with it.'
> **You:** 'From what I have learned about helping yourself to recover from this kind of thing, it is important not to try to forget the whole thing. It is better to face and examine what happened and acknowledge what you felt. Some people do this

on their own by just thinking it through or writing it down, others find it easier to talk to someone.'

They may be the lucky kind of person who, if given a kick start, then moves quite naturally step-by-step through the process. If so, you already know the kind of support that they need from others at whatever stage they are at, so do what is appropriate to support them.

If they don't seem to know what to do to help themselves or if they get stuck at a certain stage, then you can sensitively nudge them along with suggestions. You could propose some of the ones I have given in this book or use your own. But, be careful not to prescribe with a 'You should . . .'; give them options as in the example above. This may even bring up better ideas of their own about what is best for them to do. Don't forget that what worked for you may not be what they need. I tried to push my husband into academic work to make up for his underachievement in higher education, which was a deficit caused by hurts in his childhood. I did this because this kind of Compensation had proved so healing for me. But taking the same route just gave my husband added stress. He soon found other ways to make up for this deficit himself.

If this approach of gentle nudging doesn't work, then certainly do try giving the hurt person a copy of this book. If they are too upset or worried to concentrate on reading right now, offer to explain the process as simply as possible. You could then go through the Nutshell summaries at the end of each chapter with them. I suggest concentrating on the first five and just referring to the bonus steps that are available for later. Just knowing about the Strategy and having an orderly plan of action can help tremendously, as I hope you have now learned yourself.

Watch Out For Your Auto-Responses

We have looked at how easy it is to leap straight forward into the stage that is most comfortable for us. If you have a tendency to leapfrog over, for example, the Comfort stage, you may well do the same when helping others too. You should know your weak areas by now and may have worked hard to improve them. But when we are upset at seeing others' pain, the best of us will unconsciously revert to old ingrained habits, especially if these were established in childhood.

Try Using Some of the Professionals' Techniques

These are the kind that I often give to professional therapists and voluntary counsellors and coaches on training courses. I have selected some that you might find useful (*see* pages 230–33). Don't be overwhelmed by the length of the list. Just pick out one or two at a time to try. Or use them as a checklist if you are not making much progress in helping someone to move on. There may be something you could change in your approach which might make a difference. Some will take a bit of practice to get them right, so you may want to try them out first in other situations.

Use Humour with Care

Humour has undeniable healing powers, but it can also be used as a tool for denial and a repression of feelings that would be better aired. In the early stages of healing you should avoid it, even if you know the person usually responds well to your witticisms or jokes. Later, humour can be very useful when discussing fantasy revenge in Compensation and trying to establish some Perspective. The general rule is that the humorous approach is usually best led by the hurt person themselves. But don't encourage the self-deprecating kind that is rarely healing.

Keep the Small Acts of Kindness Flowing

Don't become so absorbed in your role as 'amateur therapist' that you forget to do some of the simple acts that can mean so much to an emotionally wounded person. And don't ever think that someone is so emotionally tough that they don't need these. I certainly still do! Don't hold back for fear of re-igniting a hurtful memory. Just choose your moment carefully so that they have the privacy to express their feelings and recover if necessary.

An example of a small act of kindness could be:

- Sending them a card or buying or making them a little treat from time to time, even if you are seeing them regularly;

- Picking up the phone or sending a short email or SMS message to say, 'Just thinking about you. Hope you are feeling a little better.'

- Remembering the anniversaries, even if they are fairly recent by just commenting sympathetically. For example, 'It's a month now since you broke up isn't it. It probably still feels like yesterday.'

- Commenting empathically on triggering news stories. For example, 'I was thinking about you when that man was given a life sentence yesterday. It must be hard when you see all that kind of stuff in the press.'; 'Every day there appears to be another soldier dying somewhere. That must be so hard for you when you are trying to get on with your life.'

Ask for Help Before You Can't Manage without it

Keep a very watchful eye out for the warning signs I have listed below. They are all a possible indication that a more serious problem has set in. If you spot a few of these, it may be a sign that some professional help is needed. The first person to consult would normally be your GP. But if you prefer you could go to a recommended therapist or counsellor. For people suffering as a result of a fairly major problem, there are also charities which should be able to advise you even if the hurt person does not appear interested in taking advantage of their services. It is important to remember that it is easier to persuade someone to take this kind of help before things have become so bad that they are exhibiting the symptoms in the latter part of the list.

Signs that may indicate the start of a serious problem:

- Very little sleep especially if waking early and being unable to get back to sleep;

- Severe loss of weight;

- Binge eating that you suspect may be a symptom of bulimia (bulimics are notoriously good at covering up signs of sickness);

- Staying in bed for prolonged periods in the day;

- Preoccupation with their and loved ones' health;

- Not bothering to make the best of their appearance;

- Underachievement at work, school, college or sport;

- Constant self-put-downs and substantial drop in levels of confidence;

- Reports of feeling lonely even when with people;

- Prolonged diminishment of sense of humour;

- Increasing irritability over small frustrations;

- Mistrust of people that causes relationship problems;

- Lack of motivation or excitement and disinterest in plans for the future;

- Often appearing to be disassociated from what is going on around;

- Aggressive outbursts that frighten others;

- Preoccupation with the problems of the world and a sense of hopelessness about its future;

- Obsessive thoughts and plans concerning revenge or punishment;

- Drinking too much;

- Possible signs of drug taking (e.g. secrecy; mood swings; money missing; dilated pupils or red eyes; sudden use of breath fresheners; sweating);

- Showing an increased interest in suicide or euthanasia, or doing highly risky activities without taking much care about personal safety.

There is no greater loan than that of a sympathetic ear.

Frank Tyger

Listening and Questioning Techniques

- When someone is Exploring, it is natural to want to interrupt with your own story if you have had a very similar experience. But try not to do this. If you do, the hurt person may get taken off their memory track to express sympathy with you or compare their hurt to yours. At first, concentrate on just using **encouraging noises, words and phrases**. This will help control your urge to interrupt and help them to see that you are really listening intently.

  For example: 'mmh'; 'Oh no!'; 'Really!'; 'Never!'; 'Tell me more'; '. . . and then?'

- Be conscious of your **body language** and make sure that it is also communicating that you are listening hard.

  For example: nodding; having some direct eye contact from time to time; giving a caring smile or other appropriate facial expression, and sitting or standing slightly forwards.

  Also make sure that your other body language stays in tune with that of the hurt person. Obviously you don't have to cry along or thump your fist with them but, at the very least, check that yours is not unsympathetically clashing with theirs.

  For example: not smiling if they are frowning; not speaking fast when they take their time; not sitting very casually when they are tense and bolt upright; not staring when they are avoiding eye contact.

- To gently encourage someone who finds it difficult to talk, just simply **repeat back some words and phrases** which seem (quite miraculously) to keep them talking. Don't just act like a parrot though, put them in a sentence that makes sense and is appropriate to the stage they are at.

For example, he or she may say, 'I don't know why she just ignored me,' and then stop. If they were Exploring, you might respond with, 'She just ignored you and then . . .' If they were in the Perspective stage you might say, 'You don't know why?'

- If they seem to have gone off on an irrelevant tangent (as can often happen), or jumped forward to another stage, help get them back on track. But don't confront them because they are still vulnerable. Instead, hold out your hand in an upright position to stop them and ask if you can **clarify** something.

  For example, if they were trying to Explore and have gone off track, you might say, 'Just a moment, can I clarify something before I forget? When you said just now that you felt upset, what exactly was happening then?' If they were talking through ideas with you for Compensating themselves and then digressed into an irrelevant story, you might say, 'Just a second, I don't want to lose track of your ideas, you were saying that you could book a weekend away or you might like to treat yourself to a new CD – is that right?'

- At the end of your conversation, **summarize** what you think you have heard the other person say. This is very important because when we are emotionally aroused (and if we care, we will be), we are more likely to put our own 'stamp' on the story depending on how we felt about it and our own similar experiences.

  For example, 'Can I just check what I think I've heard you say about what happened and how you felt?'

  This is also a good strategy to employ if you want to end a conversation because you or the hurt person have had as much as you can take for now, or because other needs are calling for you.

- Sometimes it can be very clarifying to use a **metaphor** which seems to you to sum up the essence of what the hurt person has said and what you think that they are trying to convey. If you are going to do this try to use one that means something to them.

  For example, 'He is supposed to be like a referee in disputes like that, isn't he? But it sounds as if he was acting like a lout!' 'You're so right. As Chairman he shouldn't act like that. Even if he secretly wants you off the project, he shouldn't have insulted you in public.'

- Ask **open questions** if you are receiving one-word replies to your questions or encouraging comments. These are the ones that start with what, why, where, when and how.

- Ask **closed questions** when you feel they are stuck and need to move from one subject to another.

  For example, you might say, 'So do you think that the relationship has now finished for good?' The other person might reply, 'Yes I do. It's over for me.' You could then say, 'I guess that means you are feeling really sad – it's been a long time.' (You would then be nudging them gently from Exploration into Expression.)

- **Verbally acknowledge the feelings** that both you and they may be experiencing. This will make it clearer to them that you are empathizing even though you know you are. I have heard so many hurt people say that when they told their story to someone they were met with a blank face and almost nil response. This may well have been because the listener was stuck in shock, or over-identifying or wrapped up in their anxiety about what they could do to help. To avoid this happening, focus on communicating verbally about the feeling. This will also help to check that you are reading their emotions right and not putting your own interpretation on them.

For example, 'Wow – I feel shocked. I can see why you are angry.' 'How disappointed you must feel – well, at least that's how I felt when I failed to get into medical school – is that how you feel? Oh really, you feel angry. Why's that?'

- **Avoid rushing in to fill every silence**. Remember that hurt people may need more time than most to think. Their memory can be affected and unexpected or overwhelming emotions may start to be ignited. Certainly don't deal with your anxiety by immediately rushing in with unnecessary good advice and reassurances, as this can stop them from doing what they may need to remember or feel in order to heal.

I couldn't bear his misery, and so I comforted him.

Margaret Forster, *Over*

HELPING CHILDREN

Helping children to heal well from emotional wounds is vitally important. Here are just a few reasons why. Festering feelings can:

- Damage their potential for learning. They cause stress which we know can affect the functioning of memory;

- Limit their personality development. For example, most of the adults I have seen who suffer persistently with confidence, chronic anxiety and relationship problems are still harbouring unhealed hurt from their childhood;

- Cause physical health problems due to the stress on their body from the tension and toxins that build up when feelings are suppressed inside;

- Increase their chances of becoming prey to bullies because their vulnerability will show;

- Lead them to become bullies themselves if they have been hurt by children or adults who have abused their superior power;

- Depress their spontaneity and curiosity urge so they don't have as much fun and adventure;

- Render them less able to deal with emotional hurt in their adulthood because they have not learned how to recover.

This list might sound like a heavy responsibility for anyone who is a parent or has a role such as a teacher, sports coach or childcare worker where they are in *loco parentis*.

I am glad I didn't compile this list before I became a parent or a childcare officer as it might have frightened me away from both roles! However, I do wish that I had known what I now know about emotional healing before I started both roles. It would have made my parenting and work with children and their families so much easier, not to mention the beneficial effect it may have had on the children.

But if you are feeling daunted, don't be. Through reading this book you have already learned enough to make a massive difference to the children you look after. If you just apply this knowledge to the healing of your own emotional hurts and you care enough to be reading this section, you will be at least 90 per cent on the way to being the perfect person to help children through theirs. After all children, especially very young ones, learn these kinds of life skills best by modelling the example of people whom they love and respect.

If you don't feel entirely comfortable relying solely on your role-modelling, the general guidelines which I gave earlier should be useful. In addition, here are a few extra.

Start as Early as Possible

On page 19, when introducing the Emotional Healing Strategy, I gave an example of how two parents helped a child recover from a minor disappointment when he was very young. I hope that gave you some inspiration and showed you how easily and naturally it can be done. You can also drop in simple messages about good healing during play and when telling and reading stories.

For example, 'Look at Jonny – he's crying. He needs a cuddle, doesn't he?' 'I think she needs to tell her mummy what a big bully that girl Lucy is, doesn't she?'

Seize Everyday Opportunities

Don't forget that everyday minor hurts provide the best learning opportunities for dealing with major ones, should they come along. A friend, Jane, after reading the first two-thirds of this book, told me that she was immediately able to apply some of her new knowledge to one such opportunity.

> *'A beloved teacher left my daughter's school at the end of term to move to another country. There were several girls clustered around her at the school gates, weeping. The teacher herself was tearful. The parents of the girls were trying to extract their children and cheer them up. I heard some mothers say, 'Never mind, perhaps she'll come back to visit,' and 'How lovely she's getting married, you should be happy for her,' and 'Come on, that's enough crying.' I immediately thought of this book and realized this would be counterproductive. I listened to my daughter tell me about how sad she was, and let her cry herself out.'*

Look for Symptoms as Well as Verbal Disclosures

Very often children (even teenagers) are simply not articulate enough to talk about feelings. You may need to prise their hurt experience gently out of them when you spot a symptom that may indicate they are suffering, such as one of those listed on page 242, or if they are very young they may display one of the classic distress signs such as the following:

- Bedwetting

- Persistent nightmares

- Jealous behaviour

- Regressed behaviour

- Clinginess

- Above-average disobedience

- Unusual hyperactivity.

Before rushing to the telephone for the number of a Child Guidance clinic, try first to find out yourself what might be wrong and use what you have learned in this book to help heal whatever hurt might have occurred. Of course, if the problem persists, then professional help should be sought, but much more often than not it should not be necessary.

Use Indirect Methods Rather Than Direct Questioning if You Spot a Symptom

Many years ago when my daughters were young, I offered to do a weekly dramatherapy group at their school. This was a primary school in a privileged semi-rural town where social and behavioural problems were minimal.

The group proved very popular, but I was only able to run it for a term. I had to abandon it because it was bringing too much buried hurt out of the closet. The teachers could not cope. While they were trying to do up shoelaces to get the children out to the playground for a games lesson, the children would start telling them all about Grandpa's death last year, Mum's row with Dad last night, or the bullying they had had on their way to school. I also heard about a few even worse scenarios, about which some children had never confided in anyone.

I was truly shocked. I had intentionally not used techniques that I thought might encourage this kind of deep disclosure. We were merely playing games and acting out everyday scenes in a light-hearted way. The children would take various different roles so that they could develop a better understanding of how other people might think and react in the same situation. At the end we would sit quietly in a circle and do some relaxation and then have a general chat together for ten minutes or so.

With uncomfortable hindsight, I can see why these sessions had been such a powerful prompt for the children to disclose their anxieties, fears and sadness. They were encouraging spontaneity and self-reflection in the context of a relaxed atmosphere of trust with a compassionate adult who was a good listener. This was enough to uncover emotional hurt that parents and teachers had no idea that the children were harbouring.

Many adults make the mistake of sitting down with a child they suspect might be emotionally hurt and asking them what is wrong. Sometimes they do this over and over again, saying, 'I know you

– you're upset about something. Why won't you tell me what it is?' To a child who may be inarticulate, confused and frightened this kind of pressure can make him or her feel 'silly' as well as sad. It can even make children feel guilty as the parent or other loved carer looks worried and upset themselves.

As I discovered the hard way, you are more likely to have success by using a more indirect approach. I am not suggesting that you qualify as a dramatherapist, but you could try, for example:

- Selecting a relevant story;

- Making a comment about a hurt seen in a TV programme;

- Looking at or drawing pictures together;

- Commenting on their play or while playing with them;

- Telling a story about something that happened to you when you were a child.

While doing an activity like this, you can then watch their reaction very carefully for body-language clues. When you start to explore with non-threatening questions and comments, do so very slowly. Help them articulate for themselves how they feel by sharing stories and using examples from their life experience. When trying to get across a positive message about healing, refer to the behaviour of role models they love or admire. These can be relatives, teachers or their hero characters from books and films or sport.

With older children, the best method is often to find a way to have some extended one-to-one quality time with them. This should involve doing an enjoyable activity together that will help the child relax with you. It could be a day trip or a night away to a beach, to see a big football match or a show. Afterwards, perhaps while you are having a quiet meal or walk together, you can start asking some general questions about the areas in their lives where you guess there may be a problem. This has been my most successful tip when I have been advising worried parents of teenagers. Often parents say at first that there are no activities which they can do together, but eventually they always manage to think of one, even if it costs some money!

Watch Out for Your Auto-Parent Responses

Because looking after children can be stressful, it is likely that sometimes we will respond to our children in the way we were programmed to do through our early childhood conditioning. If you had a problematic childhood or your parents or parent-figures were not good role models of how to heal, you may not respond as well as you would normally do when you are relaxed and have more time to think.

Another problem that may occur and which can also affect your handling of children's hurts is that what they are experiencing may trigger suppressed memories of hurts that you had at a similar age. If these are negatively affecting you or the children, heal them promptly.

It wasn't until my own boy reached eleven that I realised what an effect losing my father at that age had had on me.

Christy Moor

Find Someone Else to Help When a Major Hurt Occurs That Affects You Too

I have already mentioned in an earlier chapter how difficult it was for me to help my daughter when she lost her sister so suddenly. My problem is one that I know is common in families when a child has died or there is another kind of major family problem such as a serious illness or a difficult divorce. In these situations, try to find another adult whom they know and trust, who can spend time with them and will gently encourage them along the first few steps of healing. Plan ahead whenever you can so that this adult can start spending extra time with the child before he or she faces a big emotionally daunting event such as going into hospital or starting a new school.

If you work in an institution that has suffered a tragedy, then arrangements for a professional counselling service are now usually made. But you don't have to give over all the healing work to them. The children still need help from those with whom they have a relationship of trust and respect. You may not be able to give them physical comfort, or be their counsellor and chief confidante, but there are many other things you can do that will encourage their healing.

I recently read about some of the sensitive healing actions that one headmaster took in the UK. When two of his pupils were abused and murdered by the school caretaker, he initiated several communal healing projects for the teachers and children. One of these was to have a beautiful memorial stained-glass window made featuring two doves. On the anniversary of the murders he also initiated a ceremony when two doves were released into the sky in front of the children. Doing something symbolic such as this helps children to acknowledge and express any enduring hurt. It also gives them the permission to get any extra Comfort they may need.

Be as Honest as Possible

Don't overprotect children from the harsh reality of hurts. They need to know and deal with truths that are often considered 'unspeakable'. In order to heal properly they need to know that, for example, death is death, not sleep, and totally unacceptable behaviour such as violence, abuse and murder is a threat in the real world and not just in movies and computer games. Pretending that serious hurt only takes place on another planet won't do your children any favours if they encounter them and do not know that they, or anyone else, can recover.

HELPING EMPLOYEES OR ANYONE ELSE YOU MAY LEAD OR SUPERVISE

Once again, role-modelling is most important. It is pointless preaching good healing behaviour if you don't understand the process and practise it yourself. So, if you happen to have bought this book just for this section and have skipped the rest, you'll need to start again at chapter one!

Most leaders and managers have now heard about the concept of emotional intelligence and think it is something they should know about even if they might be unable to tell you exactly what it is. But emotional healing is another matter. They might not even consider it has any relevance to their role at all. It is commonly thought to belong fairly and squarely in the private personal realm. Even when it is encountered as a problematic issue in the confidential confines of mentoring or executive coaching, the person concerned is usually advised to seek help from a counsellor or therapist. For most emotional hurts this is taking a pneumatic drill approach when a gentle touch by a nutcracker would produce an adequate and much quicker solution. With the knowledge gained from reading this book and a modicum of compassion, you should be able to do a substantial amount to help the hurt person do the healing they need to do. But here are a few extra guidelines that I hope will make your helping role even more effective.

Consider It Your Concern even if the Hurt Happened Elsewhere

Unhealed emotional hurt is bad for any kind of business. As we discussed in the chapter on Expression, it does insidious damage to health, performance and potential. The effect is the same whether the hurt was received at home, at work or through a leisure activity. Although you may only be responsible for the person in one area of their life, it is important to be aware that unresolved emotional hurt of any kind can interfere with the workings of people in your domain. So even if it is not strictly your 'business' you have something to gain from helping the healing process along if you can. This could mean, for example:

- Offering to take someone for a drink to help them talk about their teenage son's disastrous exam results or suspected drug habit;

- Sending them a personally composed message of empathy on a card when you know their wife or husband or child has been taken ill;

- Giving them some unofficial compassionate leave or offering flexi-time, or covering for them if a close friend has died and they need to take some private time out to express and control their feelings;

- Helping them find a position in another branch or another team if they really need to move to get over the break-up of a marriage;

- Putting them in contact with someone else for whom an injury has put a stop to their sporting hobby and who now has Perspective;

- Asking, 'How's it going?' or saying, 'Hope you are still taking good care of yourself,' long after the event and until you are convinced they are recovered.

Watch Out for the Hidden Symptoms of Unhealed Hurt

> Resistance to change, the reluctance to give up possessions, people, status, expectations – this, I believe, is the basis of grief.
>
> Colin Murray Parkes, *Bereavement*

Because most people think that emotional hurt belongs in the private sphere, they will do their best to suppress their feelings. I have already listed some general tell-tale signs and symptoms, but here are just a few examples that are more specific to work or the field of leisure activity:

- Sudden drop in performance;

- Poor attendance;

- Falling out with colleagues;

- Less patience with troublesome customers or unruly, disrespectful fans;

- Inability to bounce back after setbacks or a disappointing result;

- Perfectionism or obsessive behaviour (these are controlling behaviours that can arise as a way of mastering near-out-of-control internal feelings);

- Sudden outbursts of inappropriate emotion;

- Reluctance to take praise for achievement;

- Oversensitivity to criticism;

- Doing unnecessary overtime;

- Persistent resistance to change (a certain amount is normal for most people).

Encourage Recovery for Emotional Hurts Encountered through Work or the Activity You Supervise

After a major setback or another kind of emotionally hurtful problem such as the sudden death of a respected colleague, don't expect 'the show to go on' immediately unless it truly has to. If it does, allocate time for emotional recovery later. The kind of processes you might put in place are:

- Meetings to Explore and Express feelings after a setback or bad news, before rushing in with ideas about how to use the knowledge gained from the hurt or giving encouragement to put the past behind them and look forward;

- Setting up a peer-counselling scheme which could provide mutual Comfort;

- Arranging a treat or giving an afternoon off by way of Compensation;

- Presenting research findings on how others have fared after similar setbacks to aid Perspective;

- Funding an emotional healing seminar or providing a bursary to attend a series of individual consultations.

Finally, let's not forget that we must not pigeon-hole the healing of others into certain roles that we can relate to. We don't need to be in any official capacity to help other people to recover from emotional hurt. We can do so many little things so quickly, even to help strangers, that may mean so much to them.

It would be a dream for me to live in a society where everyone felt that it was not just a duty but a pleasure to help others recover their sense of emotional stability, optimism and trust in the world.

When Laura died I had many cards and messages from readers I had never met. These expressions of empathy and Comfort and tips from their own experiences of recovery helped me enormously. Mo Mowlam, the British MP who had a brain tumour, said she also had a similar experience. She received hundreds and hundreds of letters when her story became public.

These major tragedies do move people enough to bring us together to help heal each other. But wouldn't it also be wonderful if we could all become just a little more healing to each other as we go about our everyday lives?

A week ago, I was sitting in a plane next to a woman who was sobbing as she read some postcards. We didn't share a common language, so instantly I felt powerless to help her. But I fought against this feeling and did what I could. I hope that my attempt to show compassion with a small acknowledging smile gave her a momentary piece of Comfort. It certainly helped me to feel a little better once I had decided to do something rather than ignore her distress. As this wonderful Hindu proverb reminds us:

Help your brother's boat across and you will reach the shore.

Don't forget to take the Emotional Healing Strategy's reminder mnemonic with you when you are crossing your troubled waters or taking others across theirs:

EVERY EMOTIONAL CUT CAN PRODUCE CREATIVE FRUIT

Good luck!

Further Help

If you would like to do some further reading on any of the issues discussed in this book, I suggest that you do a subject search on one of the internet bookshops. You can now browse on screen through the pages of many books. Doing this either electronically or in a bookshop or library is the very best way to tell whether a particular book could be helpful to you.

Alternatively, you could search the internet for a relevant professional self-help organization and ask them for a recommended reading list. The charity Cruse, for example, has an excellent one for anyone seeking further information or help with recovering from loss. http://www.crusebereavementcare.org.uk. This organization and many others also offer additional services such as counselling or self-help groups.

If you do not have access to a computer then your local library or health centre will be able to recommend books and relevant organizations that might be able to help.

SHORT BIBLIOGRAPHY

The following books were either quoted or referred to in this book. The list includes books by professional researchers and therapists in the field of emotional healing, as well as some relevant autobiographies and novels. Please remember that this list only represents a tiny fraction of the many hundreds of books from which I have drawn wisdom, comfort and inspiration.

Isabel Allende, *Paula* (Flamingo, 1996)

Bob Deits, *Life After Loss* (Da Capo Press, 1994)

Monty and Sarah Don, *The Jewel Garden: A Story of Despair and Redemption* (Hodder & Stoughton, 2004)

George Eliot, *Middlemarch* (Penguin Classics, revised edition, 2003)

Margaret Forster, *Over* (Vintage, 2007)

Elizabeth Kubler-Ross, *On Death and Dying* (Scribner Book Company, 1997)

Kevin Lewis, *The Kid Moves On* (Penguin, 2005)

Frank McCourt, *Angela's Ashes* (HarperPerennial, new edition, 2005)

Alice Miller, *The Drama of Being a Child* (Virago Press, 1987)

Alice Miller, *Breaking Down the Wall of Silence* (Virago Press, 1991)

Colin Murray Parkes, *Studies of Grief in Adult Life* (Brunner-Routledge, 3rd edition, 2003)

Harold Pinter, *Betrayal* (in *Harold Pinter: Plays*, Faber & Faber, 1998)

Christopher Reeve, *Still Me* (Arrow Books, new edition, 1999)

Anthony Storr, *Human Aggression* (Penguin, 1968)

J.R.R. Tolkein, *Lord Of The Rings* (Allen & Unwin, 1954)

Books by Gael Lindenfield

Many of my other books have also proved helpful to people recovering from emotional hurts. Here is a list of the most relevant titles. A full list of my books can be found on my website:

Managing Anger
Assert Yourself
Success from Setbacks
Self Esteem
Self Esteem Bible
Super Confidence
Emotional Confidence
The Positive Woman
Bouncing Back from Heartbreak
Confident Children
Confident Teens

To contact Gael and for details of Gael's consultation services, courses, books, short retreats in Spain, and podcasts please visit her website:

http://www.gaellindenfield.com